NO-CODE

VIDEO GAME DEVELOPMENT USING UNITY AND PLAYMAKER

NO-CODE

VIDEO GAME DEVELOPMENT USING UNITY AND PLAYMAKER

MIKE KELLEY

CRC Press
Taylor & Francis Group
Boca Raton London New York

CRC Press is an imprint of the
Taylor & Francis Group, an **informa** business

AN A K PETERS BOOK

CRC Press
Taylor & Francis Group
6000 Broken Sound Parkway NW, Suite 300
Boca Raton, FL 33487-2742

First issued in hardback 2017

Version Date: 20160421

ISBN 13: 978-1-4987-3565-0 (pbk)
ISBN 13: 978-1-138-42761-7 (hbk)

Library of Congress Cataloging-in-Publication Data

Names: Kelley, Michael (Computer programmer)
Title: No-code video game development using Unity and PlayMaker / author, Michael Kelley.
Description: Boca Raton : Taylor & Francis, CRC Press, 2016. | Includes bibliographical references and index.
Identifiers: LCCN 2016000237 | ISBN 9781498735650 (alk. paper)
Subjects: LCSH: Computer games--Programming. | Video games--Design. | Unity (Electronic resource) | Three-dimensional display systems.
Classification: LCC QA76.76.C672 K456 2016 | DDC 794.8/1536--dc23
LC record available at http://lccn.loc.gov/2016000237

Visit the Taylor & Francis Web site at
http://www.taylorandfrancis.com

and the CRC Press Web site at
http://www.crcpress.com

Dedicated to Mom
_____

Contents

An Overview of the Book

INTRODUCTION

The introduction contains information about conventions and software versions. It also characterizes the importance of discipline over motivation.

SECTION I: ALL ABOUT UNITY

1. What Is Unity and What Makes It Awesome?

This chapter will outline what a game engine is and the many benefits of using Unity. It will describe its flexibility, extensibility, and ability to build to just about every platform (video game playing hardware) there is.

2. File

Here, we identify the Main Menu Bar and dissect the File Button. Scene and Project are defined as analogous to, among other things, level and game. Best practices for successful workflow are described and Packages are introduced. We will create a Project named "section1."

3. Edit

This chapter introduces the Edit drop-down menu and all it has to offer. Here, we examine useful hotkeys and editor settings.

4. Assets

The Asset Button and its drop-down menu are described in detail. Assets are defined. The importance of packages and their use is explained in this chapter. We will create and edit a prefab from *Yoshimi Vs. Face Punching Robots!* We will also create a Unity account and purchase and import PlayMaker. We will save our first Scene.

5. GameObject: The Noun

The GameObject drop-down menu is demystified. A GameObject is defined as anything that has a transform value. Transform is defined. GameObjects are described as being analogous to nouns.

6. Component: The Verb

The Component button and all its mysteries are revealed. The relationship between Component and script is noted. PlayMaker finite state machines (FSMs) are alluded to. Readers will understand how Components add functionality to GameObjects. Components are seen as analogous to verbs.

7. PlayMaker Drop-Down

This chapter will inform the reader of the functionality made available in the PlayMaker drop-down menu. Important terms will be defined and readers will learn how to create a custom Layout conducive to the use of PlayMaker.

8. Window

Unity's Layout configurability will be expanded upon to include editor management functions. The distinction between Windows and Views will be made clear.

9. Help

Need help? This chapter will tell you where to find it.

10. Toolbar

Learn how to navigate the Scene View. This chapter teaches the functionality provided by the Toolbar. The "too-many-dials" problem is first introduced herein. GameObject Translation is described. Pivot points, their importance, and pivot point hacks are taught in this chapter.

11. Project View

The Project window will be shown as containing everything that is available to the developer. Additional, perhaps extraneous, functionalities such as search features are examined. Good work practices are discussed.

12. Hierarchy View

This chapter takes a look at the Hierarchy window. It serves as a list of everything that is in the Scene. We look to work-around the lack of folder functionality in the Hierarchy View.

13. Scene View

The most useful hotkeys for navigating our game world are presented in this chapter. Perspective, Isometric, and Orthogonal vantage points are differentiated.

14. Game View

The Game View's purpose in playtesting is explained. Likewise, the functionality of its Control Bar is described. PlayMaker Game View functionality is briefly alluded to.

15. Inspector View

In this chapter, we learn of the Inspector's primary function to display a selected GameObject's Components and parameters. We also learn that the Inspector View is contextual and can be used to inspect many other things.

16. Console View

While the Project View shows us everything in our Project and the Hierarchy View shows us everything in our Scene, the Console View shows us everything we have screwed up. We will investigate the Console View in this chapter.

SECTION II: ALL ABOUT PLAYMAKER

17. What Is PlayMaker and What Makes It Awesome?

This chapter will outline what a state machine is and the many benefits of using PlayMaker. It will describe its intuitive design, usefulness in troubleshooting, and extensibility.

18. Functions, Conditionals, Flowcharts, and Variables: Easy-Peasy Vocab

We won't need to learn how to program to create a video game, but we will need to learn some programming-related concepts. At the very least, we will need to learn some programming-related vocabulary in order to operate PlayMaker. We will do just that in this chapter.

19. PlayMaker View

We will pair names with buttons and describe their functionality in this chapter. We will learn the concepts that guide the construction of a finite state machine.

20. Additional Views

In this chapter, we will look at some additional Views integral to the PlayMaker system of finite state machine creation. The Globals, Actions, and Ecosystem Views will be examined.

21. Recreating CheckExistence as a Finite State Machine

In this chapter, we will recreate the CheckExistence flowchart as an FSM noting both the similarities and differences between the two modalities. We will introduce one of the most common PlayMaker errors and do some troubleshooting.

22. PlayMaker Sample Scene

We will create a sample Scene making use of the core concepts we have learned thus far. These core concepts include the use of States, Transitional Events, Actions, and Variables. The potential of both the Project and PlayMaker will be readily apparent by the end of this chapter.

SECTION III: FIRST-PERSON SHOOTER SURVIVAL HORROR GAME CREATION

23. Indie by Design

In this chapter, we will come up with some practical definitions and best practices regarding indie game development. We will look at an example of good indie game design and the lessons it has to offer.

24. Design Document

This is not a chapter about the creation of our Project's design document, it is the document itself. Comments are inline.

25. Our First Level (But Not Really)

A momentous chapter, here we will learn how to create an island Terrain, texture it, and populate it with tropical foliage. Heightmaps are explained. Terrain Toolkit is taught. We will create fog Rendering and Particle Effects and add in light, sky, and water.

26. Level Redux

The previous level is remade with concessions made to our fog Particle Effect. For starters, the Terrain will be replaced with level Terrain. We also create followGameObjectFSM in this chapter.

27. Particle Effects

Until now, we have only used Prefab Particle Effects. Here we will learn to make our own. We will also create an FSM and learn to save it as a Template.

28. Lighting

In the first installment of dealing with "too-many-dials," we will learn how to ensure that our painstakingly crafted normal maps display properly through the exploration of lighting settings. Important terms and concepts such as Per-Pixel and Vertex Lit (and their many aliases) will be elucidated.

29. Audio

Audio Sources and Listeners are taught in this chapter. Links to free audio resources are provided.

30. Moral to the Story

The previous chapters all revolve around accommodating a singular and simple game design modification; a lesson is learned.

31. First-Person Shooter Controls

Getting the first-person shooter (FPS) character to inherit physics properties, be controllable through keyboard input, further augmented with mouse responses, move forward and backward, strafe left and right, and to jump is no easy task. Unless it is an easy task. Then it is.

32. Random Spawn Manager

Through the process of stepwise refinement, a complicated task is broken into manageable segments. In this chapter, we do just that and create an FSM that will spawn a GameObject randomly at one of three locations. We will also learn how to facilitate interconnectedness by using Global Transitions to receive messages from another FSM.

33. Mecanim Preparation

Chapter 33 involves the preparation of Unity's newest animation system: Mecanim. Preparation involves importing animation assets, creating translations to enable their use in Unity, and establishing an Animator Controller (Mecanim's PlayMaker-like state machine).

34. Mecanim Execution

Chapter 34 involves constructing the animation state machine. We will learn the ways in which Mecanim is analogous to PlayMaker.

35. Mecanim–PlayMaker Integration and Artificial Intelligence

In Chapter 35, we learn how to trigger and control the Mecanim state machine using the PlayMaker state machine. We will briefly examine Avatar Masks and (Animator Controller) Layers that provide the main benefits of Mecanim: mixing and matching animations. In order to test our animations, we will create a very basic (and incomplete) artificial intelligence (AI) FSM.

36. FPS Character Model's Mecanim

In this chapter, we review the Mecanim workflow by creating an Animator Controller for our FPS Character Model. We will do some troubleshooting to ensure that our animations don't get stuck too long or too often in Transition.

37. FPS Character Model's Mecanim–PlayMaker Integration

We will create an FSM for our FPS character that allows it to mime shoot. This chapter will conclude our education of Mecanim.

38. Raycasting

In order to determine whether or not the player is able to successfully hit the enemy, we will learn the common and useful Action of Raycasting. We will create a Raycasting FSM and troubleshoot it to satisfaction. This chapter will mark our first Section III encounter with variables and the Send Event Action.

39. The User Interface

In Chapter 39, we will get a button into the Scene, configure and position it, and texture it. The user interface (UI) Canvas will be configured to accommodate multiple screen resolutions.

40. UI–PlayMaker Integration

In Chapter 40, we will learn the four-step process of using PlayMaker with Unity UI. We will get a button to restart the level.

41. Crunch Time

Crunch happens. True to real-life industry practices, we will get a whole lot done in a whole little time.

42. Build and Conclusion

In this final chapter, we will create a game from our Project that people can play. We will discuss how this first build is not the end of development, but the beginning of a process known as iterative development. We will explore possible improvements and we will say our good-byes.

Author

 MICHAEL KELLEY IS A former adjunct professor at University, where he pioneered the creation of video game development courses. He is an internationally award-winning indie developer and author of several game-related inventions. His company, Nickel City Pixels, Inc., was accepted into multiple technology incubators and is currently developing a number of IPs including *The Blind Shrine Maiden, DreamCasters' Duel, Yoshimi Vs. Face Punching Robots*, and *Star Foxy VR*. With his No-Code series of book he manifests the dream of game creation for a whole new demographic previously limited by an inability to program.

Introduction

WHAT YOU HAVE IN your hands is the fastest, surest way to realize your game development dreams. It is greater than the game development course I created and taught at university and costs thousands of dollars less. By drawing upon my experience as an educator and award-winning game developer you will be saving time as well. If you can create a flowchart, you can forgo years of study. You can make video games without having to write a single line of code. It is all made possible by Unity 3D, PlayMaker, and this kit.

Being able to forgo years and thousands of dollars worth of effort means it is easier to make games now than it ever was. But it is not *too* easy. Making games is work. Sometimes the work can be overwhelming. One of the perennial questions indie developers ask each other is, "How do you stay motivated?" My perennial answer is, "You don't." You stay disciplined. Motivation is what made you pick up this book; discipline is what will make you see it through to completion. Remember that as you read Section I (it is a little *dry*). To stay disciplined, remind yourself of the alternative: spending tons of money and lots of time, or worse yet, never realizing your dreams.

The following is a note on the practices and conventions used in this book. The first time an important concept or software-specific name appears in the text, it will appear in **bold** type. Software-specific names and labels are capitalized. Instructions are in bullets. The first time a software-specific name appears in a block of instructions, it will appear in **bold** type. It will reappear in **bold** type each time it appears for the first time in a new block of instructions.

The downloadable content provided with this book can be acquired from http://nickelcitypixels.com/noCodeBook/dlc.zip or from the results of a web search. In the section1.unityPlayMaker package, Scenes are provided incomplete; you will have to edit the Scenes as instructed by the book in order to complete them. In Sections II and III of the download-able content, the Scenes are provided as already complete (but staggered). It is recommended that you try to recreate the Scenes from scratch as you follow along with the book. Refer to the corresponding downloadable content only when you need clarification. Always remember that importing new content can overwrite files of the same name in your Unity Project, so please be careful!

The examples in this book were written using Unity Version 4.6.7f1, the final entry in series 4. It has the benefit of a proven track record and stability. If you would like to use the most recent version of Unity, feel free! The differences between the latest iteration of 5 and the last version of 4 are, for our purposes, mostly cosmetic. Any significant divergence between the two versions will be noted.

That's it! The sooner we get started, the sooner you will become a successful game developer. Let's go!

I

All about Unity

CHAPTER 1

What Is Unity and What Makes It Awesome?

The history of video game development is relatively short yet decidedly dramatic. In turn, borne of revolutionary technology and revolutionizing technology, its history has at times been cyclical. From an independent developer's perspective, its major epochs are defined by how easy or difficult it has been to complete a commercially viable game product.

The first video games were mostly proof-of-concept projects cooked up in university laboratories and government research facilities. Games such as OXO, Tennis for Two, and Spacewar! were one- and two-man affairs whose graphics consisted of simple 2D shapes. By recycling mechanics and graphics, small teams were able to churn out a glut of space shooters and pong clones. Pac Man, despite being more complex both in terms of graphics and game mechanics, was completed by Toru Iwatani and a nine-man team in about a year. Iwatani's small team created something that raked in money hand over fist, one quarter at a time, until they'd amassed billions. This was the Golden Age of Arcade Gaming.

The Golden Age of Arcade Gaming was a decent time to be an indie developer. It was simple enough for anyone with solid programming skills and a home computer to experiment with game creation. A small team with good financing could then take those experiments to market.

The Age of the Home Console, generations three through seven, was not as kind to indies. Arcades and PCs were no longer the place to play.

Ever-evolving hardware drove demand for ever-impressive graphics. More money in meant more money out, which in turn meant more money in. This money-primed feedback loop resulted in a need for ever-expanding teams of highly skilled artists and programmers. By the turn of the century, a "Triple A" title required hundreds of workers and a budget of as many millions. Arcades died out. The little guy could no longer compete.

And so, they didn't. Individuals who wanted to experiment and innovate pursued game development as a hobby. They cannibalized retail PC games, putting the games up on blocks, stripping them down, and carrying away the engines. A game engine is what makes games (and game development) go. **A game engine is a generalized software development toolbox that provides functionality typical of game development and game play**. This functionality includes rendering, networking, and physics simulation. It facilitates the development of video games by providing tools that allow the user to create levels, import new art assets, and implement additional scripts (code). By using engines and swapping out art assets and scripting new scenarios, skilled "modders" could transform a sci-fi game such as Half-Life into a tactical shooter like Counter-Strike. Impressed by these accomplishments, big-budget developers like Epic quickly realized that they could license their game engines to developers that were slightly less big. They could not be too much less big, however; the Unreal Tournament 2004 engine, for example, cost a quarter-million dollars to license. This left a vacuum that, in time, less-expensive engines could fill.

Some hobbyists came together in the realization that while they could not create a "Triple A" game, they could create a game engine. They created many game engines. In fact, DevMaster.net lists 370 game engines, most of which are free. A "you-get-what-you-pay-for" caveat applies here though; many of the engines are incomplete, their documentation is lacking, and their capabilities are limited.

One such limitation is a lack of extensibility. Updates to these game engines' functionality only come by way of an update to the game engine itself. Typical of freeware, these updates tend to be infrequent. Furthermore, by not attempting the completion of a game, game engine hobbyists may lack the foresight to anticipate a game developer's needs. Any added capability therefore is bound by the insight, ability, and time constraints of a relatively small, unpaid development team.

Free engines, typically, will lock creators into a programming language. No matter what programming language is chosen, the choice will decimate an already curt list of available programmers. These engine's art asset pipelines may be wonky too, similarly draining the talent pool of potential artists.

One of the worst limitations of just about every game engine is that each can only build to one platform. To build to a PC requires one engine, separate consoles pair to separate engines, and each mobile OS will likewise necessitate a different engine. Deciding upon an engine therefore locks you into a platform, restricting revenue. Good luck predicting what the market for any particular platform will be like once you are finally ready to release your game!

1.1 WHAT IS UNITY AND WHAT MAKES IT AWESOME?

The problems mentioned above all have a solution: Unity. As its name implies, Unity unifies the development process by allowing users to "develop once, publish everywhere." Developers are therefore freed from having to choose a single platform. Similarly, developers using Unity need not subjugate themselves to a single programming language. Unity allows programmers to use C#, Javascript, or Boo, individually or in combination. Extensibility has been crowdsourced through the implementation of a public plug-in marketplace. Whatever problem you may encounter, odds are there is a cost-effective solution in the Asset Store (one of these plug-ins, PlayMaker, allows developers to create games without having to program). Miraculously, Unity 3D can be had for the low, low price of free!

1.1.1 Unity

- Allows developers to publish to a multitude of platforms all with the press of a button

- Allows developers to program in several languages: C#, Javascript (UnityScript), and Boo

- Offers a cost-effective solution to many problems through its crowdsourced Asset Store

- Offers a free version

It is difficult to overstate how revolutionary, unique, and transformative these features are. Deciding what game engine to use was once the most agonizing decision a game developer faced. Such a choice would affect the game's chances of success as much or more than any other decision. Unity makes the decision a nearly foregone conclusion; today, it is the world's most widely used game engine (and with good reason). Along with new digital distribution models and mobile platform proliferation, Unity has remade the marketplace. Game development is financially viable for independents once again.

CHAPTER 2

File

W ᴇ ᴀʀᴇ ɢᴏɪɴɢ ᴛᴏ look at File, the first menu provided by Unity's Main Menu Bar. In this chapter, we will learn of Unity's three most important file and folder types: **Project**, **Scene**, and **Package**. Crucially, we will learn which to use when and why. We will create a Project. Briefly, we will examine building a project to a game.

This is Unity; this is home (Figure 2.1). Along the top, you will see what looks to be a very standard **Main Menu Bar**. And in many ways it is, but do not be fooled; there is a lot of powerful functionality in this Main Menu Bar and some things in it that are absolutely essential to know and understand. For example, if you click on **File** (Figure 2.2), you will see a lot of reference to **Scenes** and **Projects**. It is really important to understand what Scenes and Projects are and how they relate to each other. One way to think of Scene and Project is that **Scene is a level within a game and Project is the game itself. Simultaneously, think of Scene as a file (with the extension .unity) and Project as a folder.** Your Project's name will wind up being the name of your folder (and vice versa). Once this folder has been created through the **Project (Creation) Wizard**, Unity will propagate additional folders throughout. It is important that you not drag and drop files in and out of the Project folders in the operating system (OS) as it may wind up confusing Unity. The Unity engine adds metadata to the files and folders it creates to keep track of everything and to keep everything in its right place. **To reiterate, Scene is a game level and a file. Project is the game**

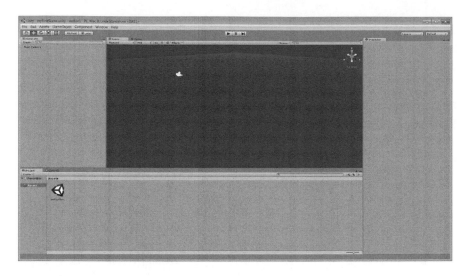

FIGURE 2.1   Unity's interface.

File	Edit	Assets	GameObject	Comp

New Scene   Ctrl+N

Open Scene   Ctrl+O

Save Scene   Ctrl+S

Save Scene as...   Ctrl+Shift+S

New Project...

Open Project...

Save Project

Build Settings...   Ctrl+Shift+B

Build & Run   Ctrl+B

Exit

FIGURE 2.2   The Unity interface with the File drop-down menu exposed.

and a folder system. **Do not move your game's files in the operating system. Always do so in Unity.**

One thing we are not really seeing yet, but is worth mentioning now, is the file type **Package**. Along with Scene and Project, Package completes the trinity of Unity file and folder types. **Package is Unity's proprietary compressed file format (with the extension .unityPackage).** It is very much like a .zip or .rar except that it contains metadata unique to Unity. **It allows you to import and export individual assets or entire Projects while retaining their hierarchical relationships and cross-references. PlayMaker, as well as other Unity Asset Store assets, is sold as a .unity-Package file. Projects and Scenes should be shared as .unityPackages. Projects should be backed up as .unityPackages.**

When you begin a game, you will first create a new Project and then a new Scene. Unity will ask what, if any, standard Packages should be imported. It is advisable to refrain from importing any Packages that are not absolutely and immediately necessary. Unnecessary Packages will cause bloat; you can always import Packages later as needed.

Some standard Packages that should almost always be imported when creating a Project are the following:

- Character Controller (part of the Characters Package in Unity 5)
- Particles (aka Particle Systems)
- Physic Materials (part of the Characters Package in Unity 5)
- PlayMaker
- Skyboxes (in Unity 5, import free Skybox Packages from the Asset Store)
- Standard Assets (Mobile)
- Terrain Assets (aka Environment)
- Terrain Toolkit

Once you have your Project and Scene created, from here on, you will be primarily opening and saving Scenes. "Save Project" saves all unsaved modifications to any asset in your Project folder. This also automatically happens when you close Unity. For this reason, there really is no need to save Projects, and opening anything other than the most recent Project will load without a Scene (no matter how many times you experience this, seeing a Project open devoid of its carefully crafted Scenes will cause you to panic). Any iterations of the game should be saved as Scenes. You do not want to have multiple Project files for the same game. Typically, you should only, have one Project per game title. Let's create a Unity Project now.

- Download **Unity 4.6.7** from **http://unity3d.com/get-unity/down load/archive**.

- Launch Unity.

- Name the Project **section1** by typing in "section1" in the rightmost section of the text input field as illustrated (Figure 2.3), alternately, by browsing to an already created folder named "section1" (if possible, locate the Project/folder on a drive other than the one on which your OS is located).

- For this particular Project, leave all *.**unityPackages** unchecked.

- Click **Create**.

- You have created your first Unity Project! We will use this Project throughout the book.

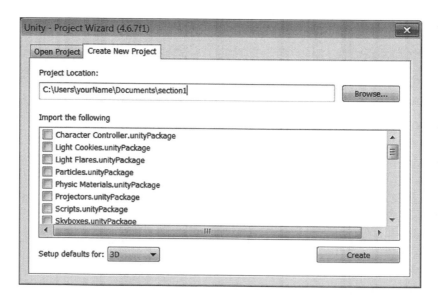

FIGURE 2.3   The Project Wizard window.

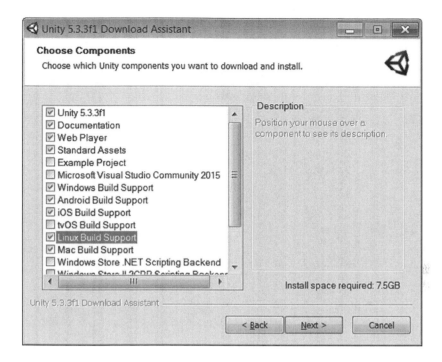

FIGURE 2.4   A selection of extensions.

The setup for Unity 5 is remarkably different. First, you'll need to download and run an assistant program, which then downloads and installs Unity. Then you must choose which extensions (aka "components," not to be confused with the Components inside Unity) to install (Figure 2.4). Once those have been downloaded and installed, you'll be given the option of creating an account/logging in or working offline. The Unity 5 Project Wizard equivalent is decidedly different as well (Figure 2.5). For one, the **Project name*** is entered into a separate field from the one in which you specify its **Location***. The default is a **2D** setup; be sure to specify 3D instead. **Asset Packages** … are chosen in a separate window. Note that there is a **Getting started tab** that leads to a video espousing Unity's features. These differences are mostly cosmetic, however, and the previous instructions are applicable.

Further along, the File menu drop-down is **Build**. Select it to open the **Build Settings** window (Figure 2.6).

Build processes your Project into a game people can install or otherwise access and play. We will look at Build Settings briefly now. You will see that you have a variety of platforms to select from. Some of

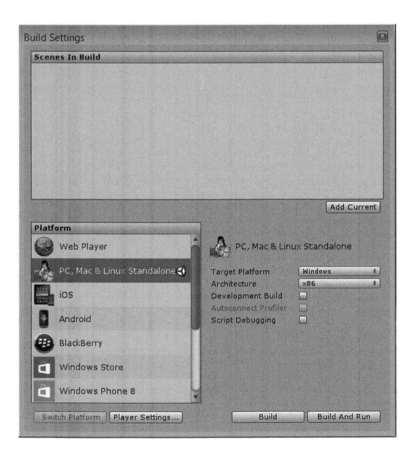

FIGURE 2.5   The Unity 5 Project Wizard equivalent.

FIGURE 2.6   The Build Settings window.

these platforms will require additional licenses. Some will require that you use Unity from within a specific operating system (e.g., you must use Windows 8 to build to Windows Phone 8). Many of these platforms require the installation of additional modules (often proprietary SDKs) to facilitate a Build. Thankfully, Unity simplifies management of requisite modules with a built-in module manager.

The list of supported devices is ever growing and ever changing. In addition to supporting new platforms, Unity will often discontinue support for older and unpopular devices.

Again, this is one of the killer features of Unity, the ability to build to many different platforms with the push of a button. Previously, publishing to a different platform meant recreating your game very nearly from scratch in a different engine. Here, you just select the platform and click **Switch Platform**. Notice that the top of this window, **Scenes In Build**, is empty. You will have to load each Scene and click **Add Current** for them to be included as part of the game. The levels will load in-game in the order that they are listed. Be sure to rearrange them into the intended order by dragging them around. You can see a few options here and many more open in the Inspector View when we click on **Player Settings**. **Note now that this means the Inspector is contextual. What it has to offer in terms of inspection will vary with what is selected. Most of the time, you will be inspecting GameObjects, but it can be used to inspect elements of the game engine itself**. Next to this, you can load images for the app's icon, name the game, define default resolutions, and so on. We are, however, getting ahead of ourselves. We will look at Build Settings more thoroughly once we have finished our game.

Build And Run assumes your settings are as you like. Unity then builds the Project. It runs the resulting game straightaway.

Exit does exactly that and provides us with a nice segue with which to end this chapter.

In this chapter we learned of the trinity of Unity file and folder types: Project, Scene, and Package. We learned that Scene is both a file and a level within the game. Project is a folder and the game itself. Iterative development is saved as Scenes; there typically is no need to save Projects. You should only have one Project per game title. Packages are Unity's proprietary compressed file format and contain necessary metadata. Unity Projects should be shared and backed up as Packages. A "Build" turns your Unity Project into a game people can install or otherwise access and play. Unity allows you to build to many different computers, consoles, and mobile devices. In the next chapter, we will look at the Edit menu.

CHAPTER 3

Edit

I N THIS CHAPTER WE will be looking at the **Edit** drop-down menu (Figure 3.1). The Edit drop-down menu may seem extensive and tedious, but learning it will help provide a solid foundation for your future as a game developer working in Unity. The most important concepts here are those of **Tags and Layers**.

Much of the Edit menu is typical: **Undo, Redo, Cut, Copy, Paste**, and **Delete. Duplicate** should likewise be familiar and self-explanatory. It is worth mentioning though that there are some distinguishing features between duplicate and a copy and paste procedure. First of all, duplicate is one less operation for the user. This may seem insignificant but as game developers, we are always looking for ways to do things in one less operation. Cumulatively, this, coupled with other transactional shortcuts, will pay huge time-saving dividends. Always remember that time is money. Another important difference between duplicate and copy and paste is that you can copy and paste across Scenes. It is possible to copy a **GameObject** in one Scene, open another Scene, and paste it in. GameObjects will be covered in detail in Chapter 5.

Frame Selected can be actuated by using F as a hotkey. If you select a GameObject in the **Scene View** and press F, it will center the object in the Scene View. Moreover, if you select an object from the textual list in the **Hierarchy View** and then hover your mouse over the Scene View and press F, the selected object will be found and centered. This is especially useful for pinpointing GameObjects that you cannot currently see in Scene View.

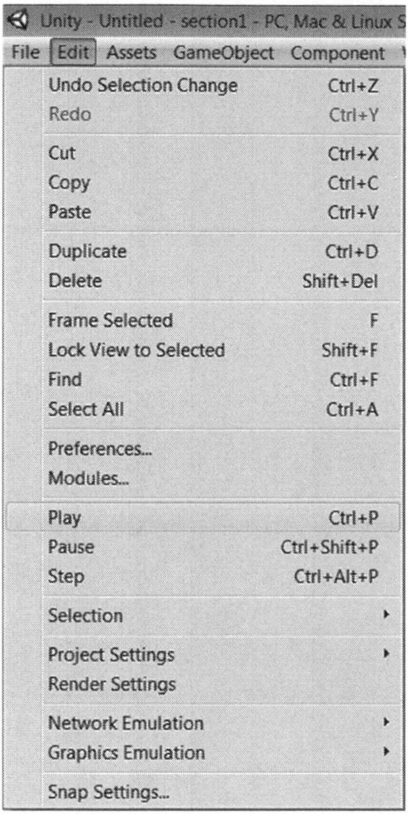

FIGURE 3.1 The Edit drop-down menu.

Lock View to Selected (Shift+F) is aptly named. With it activated, your Scene View's View will follow the object you have selected. It will follow the object unless you manually move it out of view, then the functionality deactivates.

Find (Ctrl+F) jumps your cursor to the search box of whatever view is currently selected (provided it contains a search box). It is one of the few functions that is just as efficiently accomplished by pointing and clicking, within the search fields at the top of the Project View and Hierarchy View.

Select All (Ctrl+A) selects everything in the chosen View or panel. Selecting a folder in the left panel of the Project View will select everything in that folder (but not the subfolders) for the purposes of copying items across to the Hierarchy.

In the next divisor, the first selection is **Preferences**. The options in the resulting **Unity Preferences** window define preferences for the editor itself rather than the settings of your Project. It is advisable to keep most of the default settings as they are. The exception is **Colors**. Make sure **Playmode tint** is set to red. The reasons will become apparent later.

Modules is the module manager for platform specific SDKs. Some platforms require additional software to assign inputs or facilitate a build. Unity streamlines the process of ensuring that the necessary software is present in the module manager view.

Play, **Pause**, and **Step** are used to control the **Game View**. Play will initiate **Play Mode** (playtesting) and Pause will pause it. The **Play Mode** buttons are more readily accessible in the Toolbar.

Selection occupies its own divisor. It allows you to save an object or multiple selections of objects using the hotkeys Ctrl+Alt+(number). You can then quickly access the selection using the hotkeys Ctrl+Shift+(number).

Project Settings is a menu drop-down unto itself (Figure 3.2).

Input allows you to assign inputs or reassign the default inputs on Unity's most commonly used scripts. The defaults are adequate.

Tags and Layers offers very important functionality. **Adding Tags to objects allows you to select them from the Scene's objects procedurally, that is, using code or state machine operations such as those found in PlayMaker. Layers offer GameObjects exceptionality. A layer is assigned to an object in order to either exclude or include that object in a rule specified by a script or state machine operation**. For example, if you have ghosts in your Scene and you want bullets to pass through them, you would assign the ghost a layer (in this instance, the built-in layer **IgnoreRaycast**) and then add that layer as an exception to the script or state machine operation responsible for calculating bullet collisions (in this instance, **Raycast**). We can add Tags and Layers here or more conveniently by selecting a GameObject and clicking on the Tag or Layer buttons in the Inspector View (Figure 3.3).

Knowledge of **Audio, Time, Physics 2D, Network, Editor**, and **Script Execution Order** is, for the purposes of this course, inconsequential. The default settings are adequate.

Player can be accessed through the Build Settings window and was introduced briefly in the previous chapter.

Physics, like Layers, offers GameObjects exceptionality. Physics works in conjunction with Layers to offer very specific exceptionality, that of exception

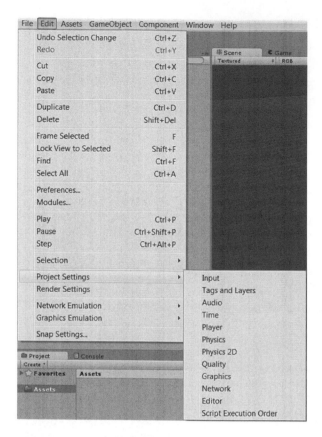

FIGURE 3.2   The Project Settings drop-down menu.

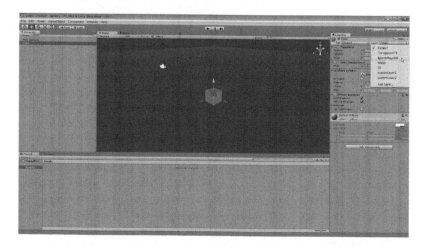

FIGURE 3.3   The Tags and Layers buttons as they appear in the Inspector View with a GameObject selected.

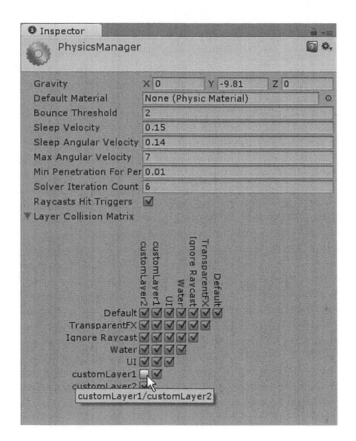

FIGURE 3.4 How to specify that GameObjects using customLayer1 do not "physically" interact with GameObjects using customLayer2.

or inclusion to Unity's laws of physics (collision). **In order to define that objects bearing particular layers will not "physically" interact with one another, uncheck the box in the Collision Matrix where those layers intersect** (Figure 3.4).

Quality allows you to specify the visual fidelity of your built game according to several presets that can be selected by the player. Perhaps the most easily overlooked parameter with the greatest consequence in the Quality Inspector View is **Pixel Light Count**. It will be covered in Chapter 28.

Graphics allows you to specify what shaders should always be included with your build. Similar to Pixel Light Count, it is an easily overlooked setting that can have a significant impact on how good your game looks. This will also be covered in greater depth in Chapter 28.

Render Settings affects how the game handles visual processing. In upcoming projects, we will be looking at **Fog** and its associated settings. We will also tackle **Ambient Light** and **Skybox Materials**. Fog causes the visuals to be obscured in direct proportion to their distance from the camera. Ambient Light allows you to tint the game rendering in order to achieve a particular ambiance. Skybox Materials renders so as to give the appearance of surrounding sky.

In the next grouping, **Network Emulation** and **Graphics Emulation** allow you to test your game under certain conditions such as fast or slow internet conditions and high- and low-Render Settings.

Finally, **Snap Settings** allows you to position GameObjects at intervals specified in the Unit Snapping View. It is activated by holding the Control key (Command on Mac).

In Unity 5, there are additional **Sign in** and **Sign out** options that should be self-explanatory. Render Settings, which will be important later, has been moved to a new **Lighting View**.

Many of Unity's Edit menu items you've seen before in other software packages. For the most part, it is important that you simply know of the options located here. Once again, the most important concepts are those of **Tags and Layers**. Be aware that there are important settings buried inconspicuously in **Quality**, **Graphics**, and **Render Settings** that will affect how good your game looks. In the next chapter, assets will be discussed.

CHAPTER 4

Assets

IN THIS CHAPTER, WE will look at the **Assets** drop-down menu (Figure 4.1). We are going to learn some key concepts and vocabulary such as **Prefab**, **Instantiation**, **Materials**, **Textures**, and **Shaders**. We will revisit Packages, both importing and exporting, and learn about PlayMaker's (free) bolt-on system for managing its extensibility.

The Assets drop-down can be accessed by clicking on Assets along the Main Menu Bar. As with most things in Unity, there is more than one way to access the Assets menu. The alternate method can be accomplished by right-clicking the right-hand pane of the Project View (Figure 4.2).

This is the most convenient way of accessing the menu. That will expand the menu and expose **Create**. Speaking of alternate access, there is an alternate way to access the Create submenu too. In addition to exposing it through the Main Menu bar drop-down and by right-clicking the right-hand pane of the Project View, Create options can be accessed by clicking the Create button at the top of the left-hand pane of the Project View (Figure 4.3).

However it is accessed, its wealth of options remains the same. The first option, **Folder**, allows for folder creation. This folder will appear in the Project View. In the next subsection, we are provided the ability to create any number of script types. Since this book is all about creating without coding, you can safely ignore **Javascript** through **Compute Shader**.

FIGURE 4.1   The Assets drop-down menu.

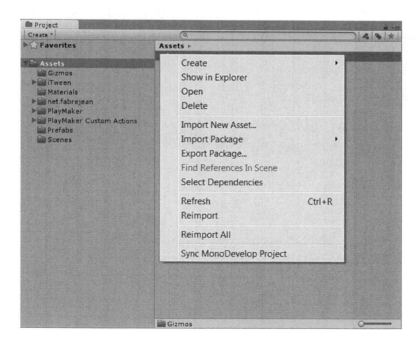

FIGURE 4.2   The alternate method of accessing the Assets menu by right-clicking the right-hand pane of the Project View.

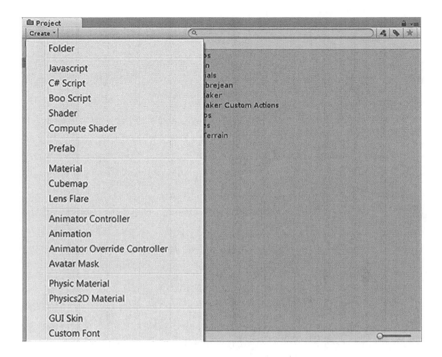

FIGURE 4.3 Clicking the Create button at the top of the left-hand pane of the Project View.

4.1 PREFABS

Further along the Assets menu, you will see **Prefab**, which is one of those all important vocabulary items. What is a Prefab? Consider a Prefab house. A Prefab house is a house that is prefabricated, that is, it will come in sections; it will already be framed and grouped together with necessities such as electrical and plumbing already partially installed. Likewise, a Prefab in Unity is a collection or grouping of assets such as meshes, materials, scripts, and other game objects that you can **instantiate** throughout the Scene. No doubt the question has occurred to you: how does a Prefab differ from a group of assets or assets that have been copied and pasted throughout the Scene? A Prefab has some very special properties. The most ubiquitous of examples is that of a lamppost game object.

With a lamppost, you might have the mesh, the material, a point light, dust motes or moths flying around, and you might even have a sound effect such as a low electrical hum. In a large city Scene, there may be a hundred lampposts. What happens if you find out later that all your lamps are too dim? If you have been copying and pasting the lamppost, you will have to go to each lamppost individually and turn up the light settings. Never mind trying to do that in one less operation, we have to find a way to do that in a hundred less operations if we ever have any hope of completing our game! This is where Prefabs and Instantiations save the day. If you have instantiated the lamppost from a Prefab, you can select the Prefab and turn up its light, and that change will propagate throughout all of the Instantiations. Alternately, you can select one of the Instantiations, turn up its light, click **Apply** at the top of the Inspector, and that change will be applied to the Prefab and then propagated. It should occur to you that **a Prefab is a special type of GameObject or group of GameObjects, and an Instantiation is a special kind of Prefab clone. A Prefab is special because any changes to it automatically update its Instantiations (clones).** Prefabs occupy the Project View and Instantiations populate the Heirarchy View once they are added to the Scene. **A Prefab is most easily created by developing the GameObject or GameObject grouping in the Scene and Hierarchy Views and then dragging and dropping its textual representation from the Hierarchy View into the Project View.** Let's get ahead of ourselves by creating a Prefab. First, we'll need to import a Package.

- Download the **section1.unityPackage** from http://nickelcitypixels. com/noCodeBook/dlc.zip (or web search).

- Click **Assets>Import Package>Custom Package** and locate and import section1.unityPackage.

- A folder named **Scenes** will now be available in the Project View. Open it and double-click **sec1Chap4Assets**.

- Select **Don't Save** when prompted; there shouldn't be any reason to save Scene **Untitled** at this point.

- The package includes a **signTastySquid** mesh from the upcoming game, **Yoshimi Vs. Face Punching Robots!**

- Select text **Main Camera** from the Hierarchy; select **GameObject> Align View to Selected**.

- Select the **Assets** folder from the left-hand view of the Project View and then in the right-hand panel, right-click and **Create>Folder Prefabs**.

- Drag the signTastySquid text from the Hierarchy View into the Prefabs folder in the Project View.

- You have created a Prefab.

- Note that the signTastySquid text in the Hierarchy View has turned blue indicating a Prefab connection.

- Instantiate the Prefab by dragging it from the Prefabs folder into the Scene View multiple times.

- In the prefab folder, click on the arrow to expand the signTastySquid Prefab.

- Select the **Point light**. In the Inspector View, increase the light's **Intensity** (Figure 4.4).

- Note that the Instances' light intensity increases as well.

- Select an Instance from the Hierarchy Views.

- Expand the GameObject's hierarchy to select its Point light.

- In the Inspector, click on the **Color** parameter and change its tint in the resulting Color window.

- At the top of the Inspector, click **Apply**.

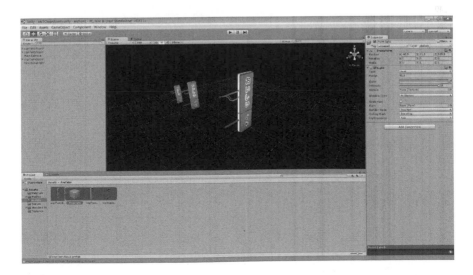

FIGURE 4.4   The Scene thus far.

- Note that the Prefab and Instances' light change color as well.

- Remember to save your **Scene** prior to exiting; recall that Projects need not be saved (they and changes to the editor/Assets are saved automatically).

- Note that this is the only time you will be reminded to save your Scene; in ensuing chapters you should take the initiative.

There are a number of things that can be done to an Instantiation without going so far as to break the link between it and the Prefab. The transform values can, of course, be modified so that the Instantiation can be moved, rotated, and even scaled. The Instance can be renamed for the purpose of distinguishing one clone from all the others. To drastically change an Instantiation or to make an Instantiation unique in such a way that it is no longer affected by changes to its Prefab, select **GameObject>Break Prefab** Instance. Doing so turns the Instance's text in the Hierarchy View black to denote that there is no longer a connection and that the GameObject is no longer an Instance. But guess what? As part of its metadata scheming, Unity *remembers* that this was once an Instance so you can always reconnect it to the Prefab. To do so, simply select the GameObject and click on **Revert** in the Inspector View.

4.2 MATERIALS

Cubemaps and **Lens Flares** are irrelevant for the purposes of this course, but it is important to understand **Materials. A Material is a collection of texture maps (Textures) and rendering instructions (Shaders). This collection does not, however, exist as a separate file type** such as a .unity-Package or .zip. Software packages all handle materials differently, but the various implementations have one thing in common: slots that you can fill with Textures. **Textures are image files that give meshes surface detail**. The term "texture" is often used interchangeably with "map." **Diffuse Maps** provide color information, **Normal Maps** tell the engine how to light the mesh to give the illusion of additional geometry, and **Specular Maps** define how shiny specific areas of the model should be. Often textures will contain an **Alpha Channel** in addition to the visible Red, Green, and Blue channels. This is often used to designate which parts of the Texture should be transparent or how shiny certain areas should be (as with Specular Maps). **Unlit** Textures (aka **Self-Lit**, aka **Self-Bright**) glow in the dark. There are many different types of Textures and most meshes will utilize multiple Textures in their Material. They will also use a **Shader**. Texture Maps define *what* should render *where*, but **a Shader provides instructions as to *how* the material should render**. A Cel-Shader (Cartoon), for example, will tell the engine to render an outline around a mesh in order to give the object a cartoony look. Instead of applying textures to a mesh individually, the textures are grouped together in the Inspector along with engine-specific parameters such as which shader to use. This grouping of textures and shader is the material and it is the material that is applied to the mesh. As a final note, if you are really desperate, you can apply materials that do not have textures and simply specify the material to be a single color. **To recap, a Material is not a file type but rather it is typically a collection of Textures and Shader instructions that is applied to a mesh to give it convincing surface detail** (Figure 4.5).

In the next menu divide are various conjugations deriving from the word "animate." Note that the **Animators** and **Animations** referenced here are *different* from the Animation and Animator Components you will find in the component section. Animations, generally speaking, are not created in Unity; they are imported and then managed using an Animator Controller. Unity's Animator animation system, **Mecanim**, is a

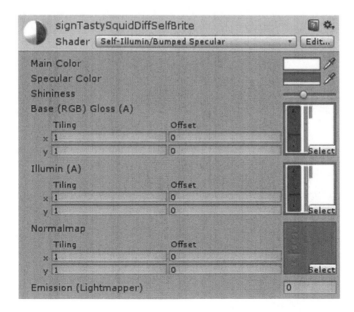

FIGURE 4.5   Example Material as created in the Material editor.

state machine much like PlayMaker. Perhaps because of the overlapping (bad) naming conventions, you have picked up on the fact that animation in Unity can be a pretty messy affair. If so, kudos. This mess will necessitate its own chapter of delineation. We will cover animations in greater detail in Section 3.

Unlike Materials, which can define how an object *looks*, **Physics Materials** and **Physics 2D Materials** can define how an object behaves "physically." For example, you can apply a **Bouncy** material to a sphere to make it bounce like a ball once dropped. At this stage, it is advised you rely on Unity's premade Physics Materials as opposed to creating your own. They are applied by attaching a **Collider Mesh** to an object and then defining its **Material** parameter. Standard Physics Materials are not created by default but must be imported as part of the Physics Materials Standard Package (part of the Characters package in Unity 5).

GUI Skin and **Custom Font** are not relevant for the purposes of this course. We will be using the **UI** system. Thus concludes the Create submenu.

Open will launch a selected asset in its default application as specified in your operating system. The operating system's specification can be overridden by Unity in **Edit>Preferences>External Tools**.

Show in Explorer will open up the selected asset's location in your operating system (folder).

If you select an art asset and then **Delete**, the art asset will be augmented with wub wub dubstep, unicorns, and rainbow sparkles. I am kidding of course. It will be deleted forever along with its Scene counterparts.

Import Asset allows you to import individual assets such as textures, meshes, animations, sounds, and scripts. This button is used quite often.

We mentioned previously how fundamental Package is as a file type. **Import Package** allows you to choose from Unity's premade Packages. Alternatively, you may browse to a folder on your hard drive that contains a **Custom Package**, as you did with sec1Chap4Assets.unitypackage. You can also import Packages directly from the **Asset Store**, one of Unity's killer features discussed earlier. PlayMaker is one such Package that you will need to purchase and import from the Asset Store (Figure 4.6). Let's do that now:

- Click the **Create Account** button in the upper right-hand corner of the Asset Store View, otherwise login and skip ahead.

FIGURE 4.6   Asset Store Window with PlayMaker selected.

- It will open up a page in your default web browser in which to create a Unity account.

- Create an Account/Log In and search "PlayMaker" in the Asset Store View search bar.

- Select the Package simply titled "PlayMaker" by Hutong Games, LLC.

- Click the **Buy** button that appears on the left side of the Asset Store Window.

- Complete the transaction by specifying the **Payment Method** and filling in all pertinent information.

- Download/Import PlayMaker using the current Asset Store dialogue.

Note that all previously purchased or freely accessible packages can be selected for Download/Import by first clicking the download icon in the upper left of the Asset Store View.

Hutong Games, the creators of PlayMaker, have (relatively) recently created a Package that in turn manages *additional* Packages for its PlayMaker Package. Why does PlayMaker need additional Packages? PlayMaker's use and awesomeness has become so expansive that it needs its own management system. This management system's name is **Ecosystem** and, along with PlayMaker, should be one of the Packages that you should import with every Project you create. It can be downloaded from **tinyurl.com/ PlayMakerEco**. You can then search, download, and find reference material for all official PlayMaker add-ons without ever having to leave Unity. With PlayMaker and Ecosystem installed, Ecosystem is opened by choosing **PlayMaker>Add-Ons>Ecosystem** (or alternately, Alt+E).

It is also worth mentioning that third-party developers have created Packages that extend or otherwise interact with Unity. For example, there is a third-party Package that bridges PlayMaker and NGUI, a popular GUI creation Package. The third-party Package then allows you to control NGUI using the PlayMaker state machine.

Note that Unity and PlayMaker are updated frequently. Most third-party Packages are not. This disparity can cause *Project breaking bugs*. I have personally experienced this first hand; once, after updating Unity, *mission critical* Packages failed to load. Manually loading the Packages caused Unity to crash. Updating the Packages did nothing. The solution was creating a new Project and updating and importing Packages *in the order of their dependency* (i.e., PlayMaker and NGUI had to be updated and imported before the bridging third-party Package was updated and imported; otherwise, Unity would crash). I first deleted all third-party Packages from the malfunctioning Project in order to get it to load. Deletion was accomplished through the OS. I then exported what remained of the malfunctioned Project as a Package and imported it into the new Project.

4.3 PACKAGES

Export Package... will allow you to export your Project or portions of your Project. This includes Scenes; the Export Package function will arrange and archive Scenes just as they appear in Unity. Additionally, it will compress the data. For these reasons you should use Export Package to back up your Projects. Do so early and often.

To back up an entire Project as a Package:

- First deselect anything you have selected

- In the **Assets** rollout click **Export Package**...

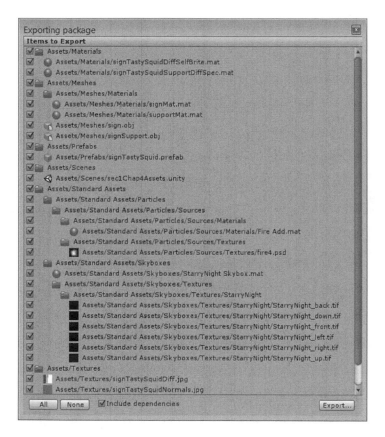

FIGURE 4.7   Export Package dialogue.

- The **Exporting package** window will appear (Figure 4.7)

- Ensure that **Select Dependencies** is checked

- Click **Export...**

- Specify a name and destination for the **Package** and save it as you would any other file

- You've created a Package!

Note that a restored Package will contain everything but your Project's name; it will assume the name of whatever Project it is imported into. To save portions of a Project as a Package, simply specify what you want to archive using the checkboxes in the **Exporting package** window.

Exporting parts of a Project is not the same as exporting individual assets. Attempting to export individual assets by selecting them in the Hierarchy View and then exporting them in the manner discussed earlier will lead to undesirable consequences. The issue being that you can only export certain elements of a Project. This means that the assets must first be converted into Prefabs. Second-of-ly, the **Include Dependencies** checkbox in the Exporting package window will have No Discernable Effect on what is included in the resulting Package. Wonkily enough, there is a second **Include Dependencies** option that must be selected from the Assets rollout menu for individual assets. As a result, the process for saving individual assets to a Package is significantly different from archiving Projects and Project parts.

To save an individual asset or assets as a Package:

- Create a Prefab from the asset as described previously

- Repeat for additional assets

- Select the resulting Prefab from the Project View

- Hold CTRL and select any additional Prefabs

- Click Assets>Select Dependencies

- Click Assets>Export Package...

- Ensure that **Select Dependencies** is checked

- Click **Export**...

- Specify a name and destination for the **Package** and save it as you would any other file

- You've once again created a Package!

It's worth repeating; Packages facilitate sharing, selling, and backing-up Projects and Scenes. The latter you should do often and with no less than triple redundancies.

Find References In Scene allows you to select an asset in the Project View and then pare the Hierarchy View text list to only those elements that reference the selected asset.

Select dependencies works as previously described. Some assets are comprised of other assets; for example, a Material is really just a group of textures, a shader, and its parameters. So, you can select the material and click **Select Dependencies** and then it will find and select the textures wherever they are in the Project folder.

Refresh functions much like a browser's refresh button.

Reimport is used if you have altered an asset in an editor outside of Unity and need to reimport it. This is only effective if it has been saved to the location Unity recognizes.

It should not be necessary to **Reimport All**. In fact, when used, it displays a warning.

Sync MonoDevelop Project will not be necessary as we will not be using **MonoDevelop**, Unity's built in coding application.

Asset Bundles is for managing asset streaming and is a pro feature only.

Unity 5 has a few more options in the Assets drop-down and the Create submenu. In Assets, there is **Run API Updater...**, Unity will prompt you to use it if necessary. **Open C# Project** replaces Sync Monodevelop in name only. None of these options are used at any point in this book. In Create, the Boo Scripts options have been removed *even though scripts written in Boo* (a variant of the Python programming language) *still work*. Shader expands to reveal additional options. **Audio Mixer** has been added. Clicking it will create an **Audio Mixer** Asset that can be edited in its View of the same name. Cubemap has been moved to **Legacy**, and **Lens Flare**, **Render Texture**, and **Lightmap Parameters** have been added. There is also a clickable **Shader Variant Collection**. None of these added options are relevant for the purposes of this course, however.

This concludes our Asset menu lesson! There is a wealth of important information to learn and review in this chapter: how to import and export Packages, PlayMaker's Ecosystem, Prefabs, Materials, Textures, and Shaders, just to name a few. We move onto GameObjects in the next chapter.

CHAPTER 5

GameObject

The Noun

I N THIS CHAPTER WE will look at the all important **GameObject** and the **GameObject** drop-down menu. We will also discuss **Local/Global** coordinates, **parent/child** relationships and learn about **Unity's Particle System**. At this stage, we are going to progress rapidly, delving into the subjects that will be relevant to our upcoming projects and touch only briefly on the irrelevant.

5.1 GAMEOBJECT

Here, we have our GameObject drop-down menu (Figure 5.1). Many of the most frequently accessed options can be alternately accessed by right-clicking within the Hierarchy View or by clicking the View's Create button. The first option, **Create Empty**, does exactly that; it creates an empty **GameObject**, which should elicit the following questions: "What is a GameObject?" "Why is this one empty?" "What purpose could an empty GameObject possibly serve?" **A GameObject is anything with a transform value. Most often, a game object is something in the game that has a physical analogy**. Transforming involves being able to move, scale, or rotate an object. So, for example, a game character, a game character's gun, and the game character's enemy are all things that can be moved, rotated, and resized. They are GameObjects. The code that allows the player to jump, the gun to shoot, or the enemy to give chase cannot be rotated, resized, or moved. Code is not analogous to anything

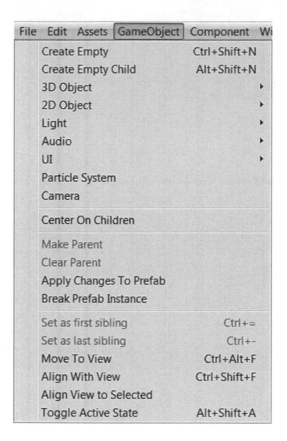

FIGURE 5.1 The GameObject drop-down menu.

physical. We cannot touch it or otherwise "physically" manipulate code. Likewise, we cannot move, rotate, or scale a sound file. GameObjects, on the other hand, can be "physically" manipulated through modification of their transform values. **GameObjects are nouns**. They are the "things" that make up our scene.

An empty GameObject has only transform values, making it very abstract and very empty indeed. It is a single point without dimension!

What purpose can an empty GameObject possibly serve? You can use an empty GameObject to define a point in space for use as a waypoint. You can use it to redefine a mesh's pivot point by specifying the mesh be a child of the empty GameObject. It can also be used to create an ad hoc folder system in the Hierarchy View. There are a number of very useful dirty hacks that empty GameObjects facilitate either on their own or through the process of parenting. Segue!

5.2 PARENT/CHILD RELATIONSHIPS

This is a good time to speak about parent/child relationships. Throughout the GameObject drop-down menu, you will see reference to **Parent, Child,** and **siblings. Create Empty Child, Center On Children, Make Parent, Clear Parent, Set as first sibling,** and **Set as last sibling** can all be safely ignored. There is a far more elegant way to create parent/child relationships, which we will do now:

- Having already saved the previous Scene, open Scene **sec1Chap5GameObject**.

- There is a red cube named parent and blue cube named child, center them in the Scene View (Figure 5.2).

- Select "parent" and add 2 to its **Y** transform value (in the Inspector View); note that it moves up slightly.

- Select "child" and add −1 to its Y value; note that it moves down slightly.

- In the Hierarchy View, drag text child onto text parent; note that a hierarchical structure results (Figure 5.3).

- You have created a parent/child relationship.

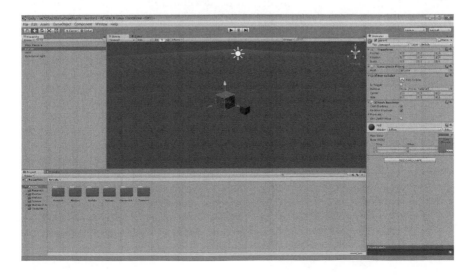

FIGURE 5.2   The Scene.

FIGURE 5.3 The resulting hierarchical relationship.

- Select child; note that its transform values are different now because it is in **local space** (i.e., the world is no longer the center of its coordinate system, the parent is).

- Select the parent cube.

- Uncheck/check the **Activation Checkbox** (the checkbox next to the name parent in the Inspector View); note that both the parent and child cease to exist.

- Select the parent and add 1 to its Y value; note that both parent and child move together.

If you stipulate the parent to be an empty GameObject, it can then serve as a new pivot point (artificial center of mass) or as the top level in an ad hoc folder system that you can collapse and expand. Of course, the child will inherit many of the properties and actions, such as deactivation, that are perpetrated on the parent. Note too that the child is now in local space rather than global space and will go wherever the parent goes.

5.3 LOCAL VERSUS GLOBAL SPACE

There are two main coordinate systems in Unity: **Global** and **Local** (in PlayMaker, **self** is used as a synonym for "local"). The best analogy for global coordinates is the objective directions of north, south, east, and west. For local, the best analogy is the subjective directions of front, back, left, and right. **Global coordinates are objective**. The center of the world is 0, 0, 0; its position never changes. **Local coordinates are subjective**. They assume that a GameObject is the center of the world. Wherever the GameObject moves to it takes its 0, 0, 0 coordinates with it. For children, the parent is the center of its world. Once the parent/child relationship is established, the child is immediately assigned local coordinates, receiving assignment from the parent's pivot point.

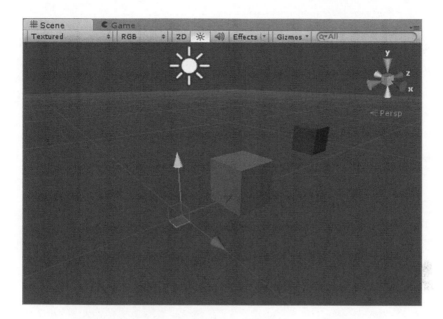

FIGURE 5.4 The difference between global and local coordinate systems.

In Figure 5.4, parent and child cubes both have coordinates 1, 1, 1. How can this be given that they are in different positions? Despite having the same coordinates their actual locations are different because the parent is using global coordinates and the child's coordinates are local, centering at its parent. The parent is offset from its 0, 0, 0 global coordinates by 1 in every direction, and the child is offset from its parent's 0, 0, 0 coordinates by 1 as well (and consequently by 2 from the center of the global coordinates).

The GameObject menu has stacks of submenus. The first of such is the **3D Object** submenu in which we have, unsurprisingly, 3D objects (Figure 5.5). **Cube, Sphere, Capsule, Cylinder, Plane,** and **Quad** can each serve as what is unflatteringly called "programmer art." These objects can be used as stand-ins until such time that the developer can import the art assets to be used in the final product.

The next divisor contains **Ragdoll** and **Cloth**. Ragdoll is a skeletal system for bipedal characters that enables the engine to manipulate the character's limbs as if it were limp, using physics calculations rather than animations. Cloth applies drapery physics to select GameObjects. Cloth is really only suitable for things like flags, curtains, and awnings. You cannot use it on anything that is mobile, mobile platforms or moving GameObjects for that matter. For example, you cannot apply it to

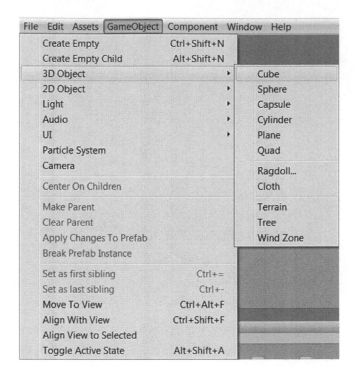

FIGURE 5.5   The GameObject drop-down menu with the 3D Object submenu visible.

a character's cape because the collision detection is just too expensive. It is best to ignore Cloth.

Under Ragdoll and Cloth is the final divisor in the 3D Object submenu. **Terrain** is, of course, extremely important as just about every game needs ground. We will look at a lot of the parameters in Terrain creation when we begin to make our FPS horror survival game. **Trees** are useful **procedurally generated** art assets. **Procedural generation is a process by which the user specifies certain parameters, and then the engine creates a randomized art asset or assets within those parameters, all with the click of a button (or two)**. In the case of trees, you can paint them onto a Terrain en masse, specifying characteristics such as the density of the forest, the color variation between the trees, an average height, and how far trees should be allowed to vary from that norm. Like height, a width average and variance can be specified as well. Using **Wind Zone**, you can designate an area in which wind will affect certain GameObjects, such as trees.

The next submenu is **2D Object** in which we have a single selection, **Sprite. A sprite is a planar image with some special properties (such as the ability to be "Sliced"). It is necessary to convert textures to sprites for use with the user interface (UI).**

The next section is labeled **Light**. Lighting is an incredibly important, often complex procedure and is fraught as well. Lighting is so important that it constitutes an entire profession within the AAA game development community. Lighting cannot be summarized in a single chapter; it will be covered in a nonexhaustive manner in subsequent chapters. The Light types you have to choose from are **Area Light**, **Directional Light**, **Point Light**, and **Spotlight**. Area Light is a pro only feature. Directional Light is a good stand-in for the sun. Point Lights cast light in about all directions for a limited distance as would a candle or unadorned light bulb. Spotlights project light in a single direction in a limited conical area.

In the **Audio** submenu, we have two choices: **Audio Source** and **Audio Reverb Zone**. You can use Audio Reverb Zone to designate an area in which you want echos to occur. An Audio Source is simply an empty GameObject with an Audio Source Component. For anything other than ambient sounds, audio files will be attached directly to a GameObject and controlled through PlayMaker.

UI is Unity's system for creating graphical user interfaces (GUIs). While it is used to create graphical user interfaces, it is not abbreviated as GUI in order to distinguish it from Unity's legacy (outdated) GUI system. **A graphical user interface uses visual icons and indicators to facilitate interaction with a software program. Panel, Button, Text, Image, Raw Image, Scrollbar, Slider, Toggle, Input Field, Canvas,** and **Event System** comprise the UI system and serve to facilitate player interaction with the developer's completed software. For example, a game's usual heads-up display may consist of icons indicating health, a minimap, and weapon reticle. It may contain clickable buttons that enable weapon selection. These elements would constitute a UI. The user interface, and in particular its facilitation through PlayMaker, will be covered in a subsequent chapter.

Particle System: At first, the vocabulary item Particle System may seem exotic but it quickly reveals itself to be an irreducible term. It is a system of particles. Particles are a series of planes that use partially transparent materials. They appear, they can move, rotate, tint, and scale, and then they disappear. Fire embers, dust motes, bubbles, snow, and smoke can all be made with particle systems.

Camera is also self-explanatory. When you create a scene, the one GameObject that is included is a **Main Camera**. Main Camera has special properties that derive from the tag "Main Camera." A scene can have multiple cameras (e.g., security cameras) but the Game View will default from the perspective of the Main Camera. Note that the Game View can alternately render a composite of the Main Camera and additional cameras (typically the UI Camera).

Move To View does just that. If you select a GameObject and click Move To View, it physically moves the GameObject to the center of the scene window. It moves the GameObject to the focal point of your Scene View. This is essentially the reverse of Frame Selected in which your Scene View moves to center the GameObject at its focal point. More often than not, you will want to move the hotkey "F" to the object. It is anticipated then that you will use Frame Selected more often than Move To View.

Align With View will move the GameObject to the coordinates of the Scene View. This is especially useful for moving a Camera into alignment. If, for instance, you like a particular vista as seen through the Scene View and you want a camera to see the same, you can select the camera and click Align With View. Your camera will assume both the location and rotational parameters of your Scene View. If it is not clear yet, Scene View is essentially an invisible camera that the developer uses inside the scene. Alternately, it may be thought of as the developer's disembodied eyes, with transform values but without dimension. **Align Scene To View** does the reverse of Align With View. **Toggle Active State** essentially turns GameObjects on and off. This is also accomplished with the first checkbox that appears in the Inspector View next to the GameObject's name, previously mentioned as the Activation Checkbox.

Unity 5 has a few more options under Light and UI submenus. These include, but are not limited to, **Light Probe Group** and **drop-down**.

Thus concludes the chapter on the GameObject drop-down menu! We learned the very important concept that GameObjects are "things." They are analogous to real-world matter; think of them as the nouns of our game. We learned several uses for empty GameObjects (waypoints, pivot points, ad hoc folders), and the process by which parent/child relationships are established. The difference between global and local coordinate systems was explained. Global coordinates are objective; local coordinates are subjective and relate to individual GameObjects. We talked about Lights. Terrain and trees were briefly introduced. Particle Systems and cameras were discussed. Finally, we learned some important align commands. In the next chapter, we will learn how to enable our nouns with verbs.

CHAPTER 6

Component

The Verb

I N THIS CHAPTER, WE are going to look at the also all-important **Component**. We will learn that they are the verbs that make GameObjects go. We will make one such GameObject, a Sphere, do just that. We will learn about **Parameters** and how they can be used to make things go better.

6.1 COMPONENTS

Up next is our **Component** drop-down menu (Figure 6.1). Components can be chosen from here. The alternate method of access is to select a GameObject and then click **Add Component** in the Inspector. This is the most convenient and useful way of adding Components; the dialogue adds search functionality. Using either method elicits a long list of options, each with a submenu. Many of the submenus are themselves a long list of options. It is not important to memorize each of these elements and all of their respective functionalities. Many times, the Components' functionality is described by its name in such a way as to make its purpose self-evident. It is important, however, to understand the concepts governing Components. If GameObjects are nouns, **Components are verbs. They give GameObjects functionality, allowing them to act**. As verbs, unlike their noun counterparts, Components do not have a physical analog. **Components are scripts, mini programs, that exist as**

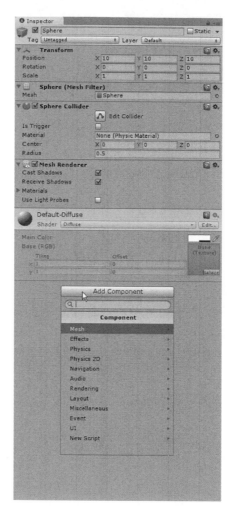

FIGURE 6.1 Component drop-down menu's alternate access in the Inspector View.

attachments to GameObjects. With a GameObject selected, its Components will be visible in the Inspector View. In fact, this is the primary use of the Inspector View, to add, subtract, adjust, and otherwise inspect the Components attached to a GameObject. Let's do that now:

- Open Scene **sec1Chap6Component**.

- Select **Main Camera** and from the **GameObject** menu, select **Align View to Selected** if necessary.

- On the **Main Toolbar**, press **Play** (Figure 6.2).

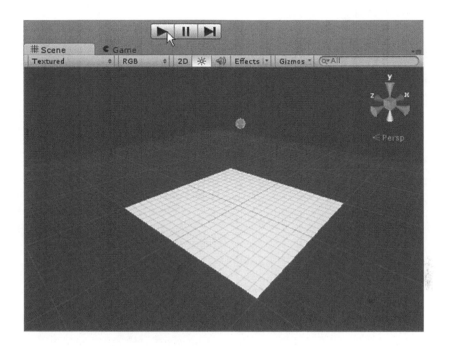

FIGURE 6.2   Main Toolbar with the cursor over the Play button.

What happened? The Scene View was toggled with the **Game View** and the rest of Unity was tinted red (if it was not, go to **Edit>Preferences>Colors** and specify Playmode tint as red as advised previously). You are no longer viewing your game as a developer but as a player. Game View displays how your Scene (level) will look and behave when played. But what happened to the Sphere? Nothing. The Sphere currently has only four Components, none of which provide any real functionality other than the functionality to be seen (**Mesh Renderer**). While Scenes come with gravity by default, the Sphere actually lacks the ability to be affected by gravity! Let's change that.

- On the **Main Toolbar**, press **Play** to exit Game View.

- With the Sphere selected, click **Add Component** in the Inspector View.

- Select **Physics>Rigidbody** (In Unity's these are obtained from the characters package).

- On the **Main Toolbar**, press **Play**.

Now, the Sphere falls! It falls unsatisfactorily however. Fortunately, Components often have many parameters that can be modified.

Parameters are values that help inform a script's behavior. They are assigned before the game runs and remain unchanged as the software executes. Let's modify a parameter to make the Sphere's physics more satisfying:

- On the **Main Toolbar**, press **Play** to exit Play Mode.

- Select **Assets>Import Package>Physics Materials** and choose **Import**.

- Select the **Sphere** and in the Inspector View, locate the **Sphere Collider** Component.

- To the left of the **Material** parameter field **None (Physic Material)**, click the target icon (Figure 6.3).

- In the **Select Physic Material** window, choose **Bouncy**.

- On the **Main Toolbar**, press **Play**.

You may have expected the Sphere to bounce, which it did. What should have been unexpected, however, is that it continued to bounce higher and higher. You can address this by modifying yet another Parameter, **Drag**, in the Rigidbody component.

GameObjects are inanimate. In order to do anything, including something so simple as to be seen or to be affected by gravity, they need Components. Components can be fine-tuned through their parameters.

As mentioned, most Components' functions are described by their names. Components are all well documented (their documentation can be easily obtained by clicking the **Help** icon toward the upper right-hand corner of the added Component's panel in the Inspector). For these reasons, it would be folly to describe all the Components that come with Unity.

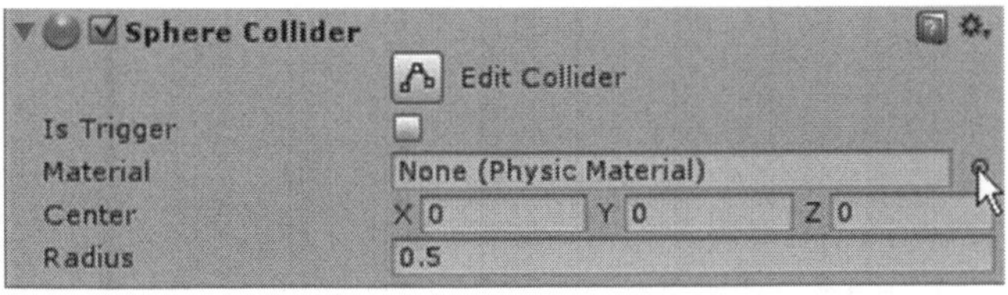

FIGURE 6.3   The target icon being selected.

Do be aware, however, of the most commonly added Components' respective groupings:

- Character Controller (Standard Package)

- Physics

- Audio

- Miscellaneous

- UI

Unity 5 functions in much the same way. Be aware though that as previously mentioned, premade Physics Materials are part of the Characters package.

In this chapter, we learned about Components and Parameters and put both to use in order to simulate a bouncing ball. We learned that Components are scripts (code) that you attach to GameObjects in the Inspector View. We looked at some of the more useful and therefore more common Component types. In the next chapter, we will visit the PlayMaker drop-down menu.

CHAPTER 7

PlayMaker Drop-Down

I N THIS CHAPTER, WE will look at the options presented by the PlayMaker drop-down menu (Figure 7.1). We will learn some important terms and manipulate the views to create a **Layout** conducive to PlayMaker's use. You are free to create your own Layout of course, but the following is optimal for the purpose of following along with the book.

Having imported the PlayMaker Package in Chapter 4, the word **PlayMaker** now appears along the Main Menu Bar. Expanding the PlayMaker window elicits many options, though the majority of PlayMaker's functionality is more efficiently accessed in the PlayMaker Views. Speaking of which, the first option is **PlayMaker Editor** (aka PlayMaker View). Where to place the PlayMaker View is a matter of preference but this book will use the Layout created as follows:

- Make room for PlayMaker by dragging and dropping the Project View tab so that it docks to the left of the Hierarchy View.

- Select **PlayMaker>PlayMaker Editor**.

- The PlayMaker Editor View will float in the foreground as will the **Welcome To PlayMaker** window.

- Choose whether or not the Welcome to PlayMaker window should **Show at Startup** and close the window.

- Drag and drop the PlayMaker Editor View so that it docks to the left of the **Console View**.

FIGURE 7.1 The PlayMaker drop-down menu.

- If you have not already, download and import **Ecosystem**.

- Select **PlayMaker>Addons>Ecosystem (Alt+E)**.

- Drag and drop the **Ecosystem View** so that it docks to the right of the Console View.

- Select **PlayMaker>Editor Windows>Action Browser** (aka Actions View).

- Note that sometimes Actions View will not appear unless PlayMaker View is selected first.

- Drag and drop the **Actions View** so that it docks to the right of the **Inspector View**.

- Select **PlayMaker>Editor Windows>Global Variables** (aka Globals View).

- Drag and drop the **Globals View** so that it docks to the right of the Actions View.

- Click **Window>Layouts>Save Layouts**.

- Dial down the slider in the right-hand panel of Project View so that the icons are of minimal size.

- In the resulting window, type in "playMakerLayout" and click on the Save button (Figure 7.2).

- You have just created a Layout!

After PlayMaker Editor, the next option is **Editor Windows**, which has already been explored in the creation of our PlayMaker Layout. There will not be an occasion to access any of the remaining Editor Windows through this PlayMaker drop-down menu.

The next option is **Components**. PlayMaker adds functionality to a GameObject much like a Component does. It should be no surprise then that each PlayMaker finite state machine (FSM) added to a GameObject shows up as a Component in the Inspector View (Figure 7.3).

Add FSM To Selected Objects is the first step in creating a finite state machine that will make your GameObject go. FSMs are more efficiently added to GameObjects by selecting a GameObject, right-clicking in the PlayMaker View's Graph view (the dark gray panel), and choosing **Add FSM. Add PlayMakerGUI To Scene** is unnecessary; it gets added to the scene automatically. It does not get more efficient than that!

The next option tree's trunk is **Tools**. The first item can be safely ignored; there is very little need to **Load All PlayMaker Prefabs In**

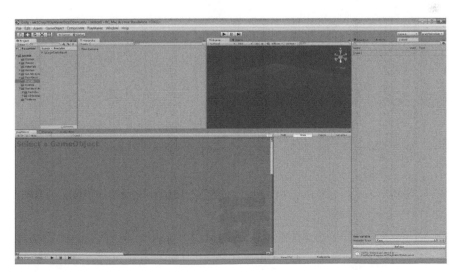

FIGURE 7.2 The completed custom PlayMaker Layout.

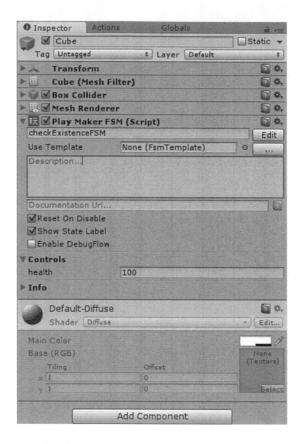

FIGURE 7.3   Example of an FSM as an attached component.

Project. Custom Action Wizard assists programmers who script additional **Actions** for PlayMaker. Many Custom Actions are available in the PlayMaker forums. **Export Globals** and **Import Globals** allow you to use **Globals** across Projects. Variables and Global Variables will be explained in a later chapter, as will Actions. **Documentation Helpers** is a wizard that "generates the screenshots and html required to document (custom) actions in the online wiki." **Run AutoUpdater** will update PlayMaker to the latest version and **Submit Bug Report** allows you to do just that.

By now, you have noticed that most of the Main Menu Bar options' names explain their functionality. This is good practice and something to remember when it comes the time to name Components, Variables, PlayMaker FSMs, and other Project parts. Case in point, **Online Resources** will connect you to online resources. All of these options, **Hutong Games**, **Online Manual**, **Video Tutorials**, **YouTube Channel**, **PlayMaker Forums**, and **Release Notes**, are meant to connect you with the resources you need to operate PlayMaker competently (though the best resource is already in your hands). As mentioned before, PlayMaker Forums in particular is useful; many Custom Actions can be found here generously donated by fellow PlayMakers.

The Welcome Screen has been covered previously. If you have deselected Show at Startup and need to access the Welcome Screen window again, it is available here.

In **Upgrade Guide**, you will find information about the currently installed PlayMaker version and any compatibility issues it may have with Unity. Conversely, you will find information about the recent Unity versions and any associated compatibility issues they may have with PlayMaker. Be sure to heed the warnings.

About PlayMaker will give you version information and a list of the good people at Hutong Games, purveyors of fine finite state machine technology, who have made PlayMaker possible. Additionally, there are links to **Release Notes** and, once again, the **Hutong Games** website.

After the divisor, **Addons** is listed. As previously noted, PlayMaker's own extensibility manager, Ecosystem, is exposed here. While Ecosystem is accessed through Addons, any subsequent addons and their documentation are in turn accessed through Ecosystem. The exceptions are **BlackBerry Add-on** and **Windows Phone 8 Add-on**, which launch directly into the Asset Store View. Like all other additional PlayMaker Packages developed by Hutong Games, both are free to download and import.

The most important aspect of this chapter was the creation of our Custom Layout. Be aware of the options available through the PlayMaker drop-down menu. The most important aspects of PlayMaker, however, are amassed in the Views we have chosen to appear in the Layout. These will be covered in Section II. The next chapter is a crash course in Windows.

CHAPTER 8

Window

In this chapter on **Window**, we will look at the distinction between windows and Views. Some of Unity's Layout configurability will be briefly revisited. Layout management will be addressed, as will be the remainder of Views.

The drop-down menu **Window** is a bit of a misnomer as everything contained within it is actually, strictly speaking, a View (Figure 8.1). The terms windows and Views are often used interchangeably, however. In addition to having the ability to be opened, closed, resized, and repositioned, a View has a tab and can be docked. A window can be opened, closed, resized, and repositioned, but it has no tab and cannot be docked.

When not docked, a View or window is said to be "floating." With multiple Views floating around, it is inevitable that they will eventually overlap, obscuring the other. **Next Window** will select the overlapped View. **Previous Window** will select the previously overlapping View.

The item in the next divisor, Layouts, was explored in the previous chapter. Here, you have the option to select from several preconfigured Layouts and any custom Layouts you have created. As seen previously, you can Save Layouts and Delete Layouts. Finally, if things get really out of hand, you can select **Revert Factory Settings** to roll back Unity to a simpler, trouble-free time.

It is advised that you back up custom Layouts. Since a Layout is not an asset, it cannot be backed up as part of a package. It can be located and duplicated through your OS however.

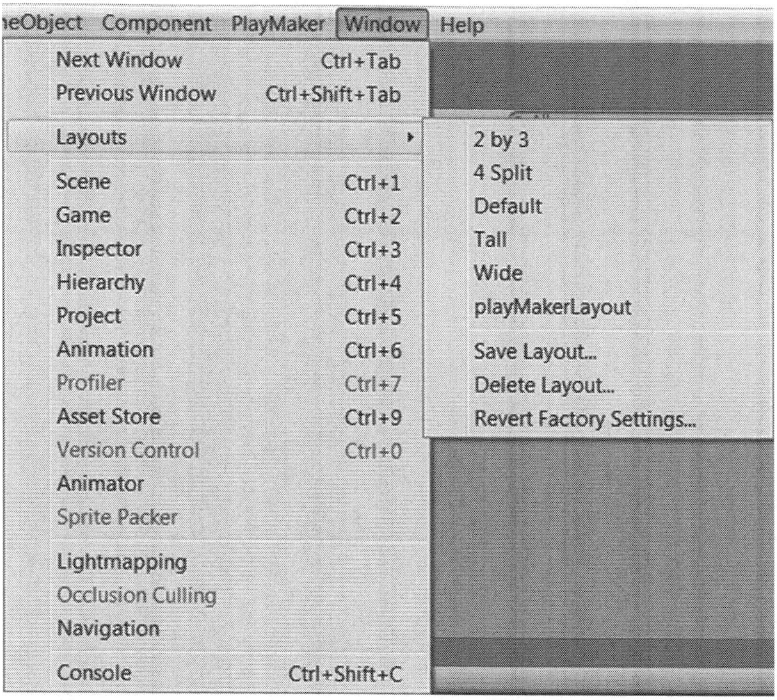

FIGURE 8.1   The Window drop-down menu with the Layouts submenu exposed.

- In Windows (the OS, not the Unity menu), select **Start>Control Panel>Appearance and personalization>Folder Options>View.**

- Uncheck **Hide extensions for known file types.**

- Download **Agent Ransack** from **tinyurl.com/agentRansack** for free.

- After scanning it for malware, install and run Agent Ransack.

- In Agent Ransack's **File name:** field, type *.wlt**, which is the extension for **Layouts.**

- In Agent Ransack's **Look in:** field, select **Local Hard Drives.**

- **playMakerLayout.wlt** should return as a result; right-click it and select **Copy.**

- Create/open a backup folder from within windows, select the negative space within its window, right-click, and select **Paste.**

When you have occasion to reuse the Layout in a fresh install of Unity, you can use Agent Ransack or another file-finding application to locate where Unity Layouts are stored. Once again, this is accomplished by using the search term "*.wlt" and navigating to the relevant file location within Unity (typically, this path is "**C:\Program Files (x86)\Unity\Editor\Data\ Resources\Layouts**"). You would then copy and paste the **playMaker-Layout.wlt** (or other custom Layout file) from the backup location to the appropriate folder within Unity as identified through the file search procedure delineated earlier. While the rule is not to move files into and out of Unity using your OS, Layouts are the exception.

In keeping with a theme of exceptions, the view selection hotkeys (e.g., Ctrl+1) are an exception from the advice that you use hotkeys whenever possible. It is typically necessary to select something from a View using your cursor, and this action does the double-duty of selecting the View as well. As a result, hotkey selection of Views becomes redundant, perhaps even slowing. That being said, should you determine otherwise from personal experience, the hotkeys are listed here in the Windows drop-down menu along with all of Unity's standard Views (note once again that PlayMaker Views are selected from the PlayMaker drop-down). We have worked inside many of the Views listed here already. The most useful of these Views will be discussed in greater detail in upcoming chapters. Those Views that are irrelevant to our objectives will be touched upon only briefly now.

Animation is a part of Unity's legacy animation system. It is still occasionally useful for syncing sounds with animations.

Profiler is used to analyze a game's performance in terms of computational resources. It allows a developer to test game performance on other devices that share the editor's local network.

Version Control helps development teams share resource in such a way that everyone is able to use the latest code. It requires a team license, use of a server, and client configuration in Unity through Edit>Project Settings>Editor menu.

Like packing clothes more tightly into a suitcase in order to save space, **Sprite Packer** packs 2D images more closely together to save on resources. It is grayed out and unusable by default but can be enabled through **Edit>Project Settings>Editor**.

One of the most resource intensive processes you can demand of a game engine is to have it render lighting effects as the game is being played. It is much more efficient for the developer to calculate the lighting effects and "bake" them (create a texture map) ahead of time. The resulting texture map cheat sheet can then tell the game how to light a scene. The upshot is computational resource savings, savings, savings! This process is accomplished in the **Lightmapping** View.

Occlusion Culling is a Unity Pro only feature that determines what the player can see and eliminate what is occluded (blocked from view) from its rendering routine. After all, if it cannot be seen, why draw it? This too saves on resources.

By now, you have undoubtedly noticed a pattern. The Views dedicated to optimizing performance are being glossed over. While many programmers consider it heresy not to optimize code, game developers consider it pragmatic. Our singular driving impulse is to "finish" our game's development. All other concerns must be cast aside for the time being, letting that which does not matter truly slide.

Like Lightmapping, **Navigation** View allows the developer to precompute an otherwise resource intensive task. In the instance of Navigation, what is being "baked" is the process of pathfinding. Many games will need GameObjects to be able to get from one side of a map to another. This is easier said than done. A nonplayable character (NPC) has to be able to determine all possible paths and then "decide" on the best path according to variable criteria. There will also be occasions when the choices the NPC makes should be randomized and perhaps even faulty. These processes necessitate a relatively complex AI system. The aim of a well-engineered engine though is to provide the types of functionality commonly needed by developers, and pathfinding is one such need. Unity, being a well-engineered engine, therefore provides this relatively complex functionality in Navigation View.

Unity 5 has a drop-down between PlayMaker and Window: **Mobile Input**. It has two settings, Enable and Disable. The Unity 5 Window menu has additional Views as well. These include **Audio Mixer Editor Tests Runner** and **Animator Parameter**.

In this chapter, we looked at the distinction between windows and Views. Some of Unity's Layout configurability was revisited. Layout management was addressed. Like any indie game developer worth their salt, we glossed over anything to do with optimization!

CHAPTER 9

Help

I**N THIS CHAPTER, WE** will look at **Help**: what is available and where to find it. Version and licensing information are available here. Help is where license management takes place.

Help offers informational resources but also helps you to manage your software and any additional licenses (Figure 9.1). The first choice, **About Unity**, launches a window showing your version of Unity. It displays a continuing scroll of the Unity development team and lists the other technologies, such as the Mono Project, which have been integrated into Unity.

In the lower right-hand corner, the **License type** for Unity and any additional platform publishing licenses are displayed. The absence of a license for a particular platform in this list does not necessarily mean that publication to that platform is prohibited; many platforms do not require a license. Note that these additional licenses are for use of Unity's additional publishing packages. They are issued by Unity rather than the platform owners themselves. Copyright information as well as the installation's unique **Serial number** is also found here.

Manage License quite fittingly opens the window **License Management**. This window offers several buttons for pressing: **Check for Updates**, **Activate New License**, **Return License**, **Manual Activation**, and **Unity FAQ**. Next to each button is a succinct and serviceable description. It is safe to gloss over these descriptions until a need to read arises. Be aware, however, that in order to activate an in-use Unity license on another computer or laptop, it must first be returned. This process is a form of copyright protection.

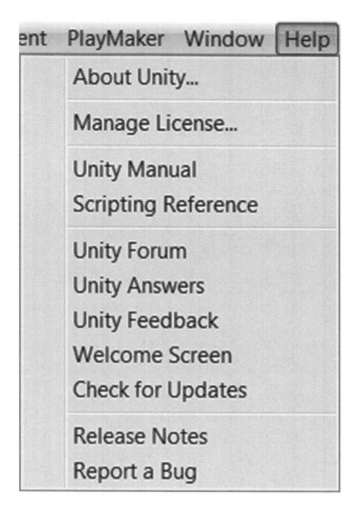

FIGURE 9.1 The Help drop-down menu.

Unity Manual opens an *offline* copy in the operator's default browser. **The Unity Manual that is opened through Unity is typically the best reference as it will match your version**. The most up-to-date manual can be found at: http://docs.unity3d.com/Manual/index.html. Of course, if you don't have the latest Unity version (not always a bad thing), the Unity Manual is bound to reference features lacking in your installation.

Scripting Reference exists alongside the Unity Manual. It provides reference for scripting. Often, in transitioning from "HelloWorld" code examples to real-world usage, novice programmers will encounter and be intimidated by code they have never seen before. Typically, this unencountered code consists of class, function, and variable names specific to the software they are developing for. The unencountered code is not something the novice programmer is expected to know; it is something he or she is expected to learn. Code that is specific to Unity is learned from studying Scripting Reference.

The reference materials will not always anticipate what knowledge is needed to complete a specific task. They certainly will not anticipate solutions to software bugs. If you encounter a problem in Unity, chances are good that someone else has encountered it first. Chances are fair to middling that someone has even posted a solution. The best places to look for such solutions are in **Unity Forums** and **Unity Answers**.

The Unity developers are always looking for suggestions as to how Unity can be improved. If you have a notion about how to make the world's best engineered engine even better, be sure to click on **Unity Feedback**. This will launch Unity's online feedback management system in your default browser. In addition to giving suggestions, you can view, vote up, and socialize other users' suggestions.

Did you hastily uncheck "Show at Startup" and regret it ever since? Hope is not lost! You can bring the **Welcome Screen** back from within the Help drop-down menu. Welcome Screen!

Back up your Project as a Package before daring to **Check for Updates**. Similarly, it is advisable that you also research compatibility issues with any third- and especially fourth-party Packages. Check the Unity Forums as well as official documentation for incompatibility issues. If you feel that the value of the additional or updated features outweighs the Project-breaking risks, click Check for Updates.

Release Notes will take you online to information regarding the differences between the latest version of Unity and the previous version of Unity. When weighing the pros and cons of attempting a Unity update, Release Notes proves an invaluable resource.

You just had to have the newest, shiniest version of Unity, didn't you? You didn't follow any of the earlier advice, did you? You just clicked on "Update" like you didn't have a care in the world. Welcome to **Report a Bug**. If in the course of normal operations you encounter a problem with Unity, you should report the problem to its developers. Report a Bug will launch the **Unity Bug Reporter** questionnaire, prompting you to "describe the problem in as much detail as possible." Note that in addition to the details you provide, Unity automatically collects information about your OS and running applications. If you are OK with this and feel that you have filled out the form adequately, click **Send Error Report**.

Otherwise, reedit or abort by clicking **Don't Send**. The Unity developers' bug-squashing efforts are very proactive. Reporting bugs will help ensure that you and your fellow developers encounter fewer and fewer problems throughout the version's life cycle.

Not much has changed in the way of help since Unity 4. In Unity 5, **Unity Connect** takes you to a web page that explains Unity Services.

In this chapter, we looked at **Help**. License management was discussed. We learned that upgrading Unity shouldn't be treated as a foregone conclusion; upgrading can have dire consequences. Doing so should only result as a decision well-informed of the pros and cons.

CHAPTER 10

Toolbar

Though diminutive, the **Toolbar** is comprised of many commonly used tools: Transform Tools and Playback buttons. In this chapter, we will look at the functionality provided by the Toolbar and hotkey selection. We will learn about the **too-many-dials** problem. We will learn how to translate (aka move or position), rotate, and scale GameObjects. We will learn the importance of pivot points and how to reassign a pivot point's location inside Unity.

We have completed our tour of the Main Menu Bar and have moved onto the Toolbar (Figure 10.1). There are a number of icons, buttons, and drop-down menus here along the top. The icons in the first grouping are known as the **Transform Tools** (Figure 10.2). From left to right, these tools are known as **View, Translate, Rotate,** and **Scale**.

View Tool, which is the hand icon, functions as if to grab the Scene and move it around. It helps you to navigate the Scene. Like all of the Transform Tools, it is woefully inefficient to activate the View Tool through icon interaction. Even its hotkey "Q" is not the best option for activation. **The View Tool is most easily activated while in the Scene View by holding down the mouse scroll wheel**. Holding the Alt key will swap the hand icon with an eye icon. This allows you functionality that, for practical purposes, is similar to **rotating the scene. This functionality is more easily accessed by (first releasing the middle mouse button if necessary and) pressing and holding the right mouse button**. If, while the hand icon is active, you first press "Alt" and then press and hold the right mouse button, a magnifying glass icon will appear. While this is most commonly associated with "zoom" functionality, in reality, it allows you to dolly your

FIGURE 10.1   The Toolbar.

FIGURE 10.2   The many icons of the Transform Tools.

FIGURE 10.3   The Move Gizmo.

view around the Scene. With all things View Tool, it has much more ergonomic activation; **the scroll wheel button can also be used to dolly your view of the Scene**.

A visual approach to GameObject positioning, the Translate Tool allows you to move GameObjects along the x, y, and z axes in the Scene View. It is best activated using the hotkey "W." When activated in conjunction with a selected GameObject, a **Move Gizmo** appears (Figure 10.3). The colored arrows of the Gizmo each represent a different axis along which to move the selected GameObject. When an arrow is selected, it highlights.

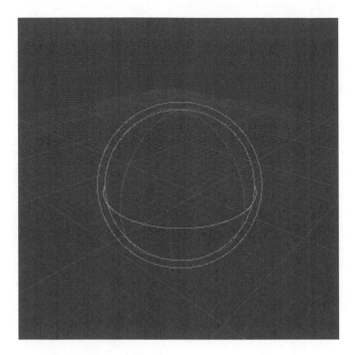

FIGURE 10.4   The Rotate Gizmo.

Subsequent movement, accomplished by a click and drag motion, is constrained along the corresponding axis (x is red, y is green, z is blue). You can move a GameObject along multiple axes simultaneously by selecting the arrows' nexus but it is not recommended.

To Rotate a GameObject, first activate the Rotate Tool with the hotkey "E" (note that the Transform Tool hotkeys exist one after the other in the same order as their icons). A **Rotate Gizmo** appears (Figure 10.4). Colored longitudinal and latitudinal lines correspond to x, y, and z axes. Selection of a line will constrain rotation to its corresponding axis and rotation is accomplished by a click and drag motion. Free rotation (rotation in multiple axes simultaneously) is possible but discouraged.

The Scale Tool, used for resizing GameObjects, is activated with the hotkey "R." A **Scale Gizmo** will appear, complete with its own colored axes (Figure 10.5). The Scale Tool can be distinguished from the Translate Tool by its cube termini. Scaling a GameObject in a single dimension can be accomplished by selecting an axis and performing a click and drag motion. Unlike other Transform operations, you will usually want to scale uniformly (in multiple axes simultaneously). This is accomplished by

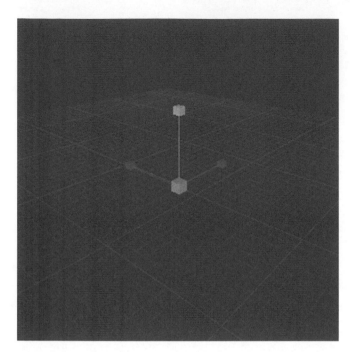

FIGURE 10.5   The Scale Gizmo.

selecting the nexus and dragging. In addition to resizing the GameObject, Scale resizes the GameObject's coordinate system as well. This means that any children of a scaled GameObject will also become relatively larger or smaller. The child's transform values, however, will not reflect its change in size (because it is in local space) unless the parent/child relationship is broken.

The phenomenon mentioned above provides us with a nice segue into a discussion of the **too-many-dials** problem. The "too-many-dials" problem results from having one value that is controlled by several sometimes competing and conflicting settings. Maybe you have encountered this problem when trying to turn up the volume on your computer. You may have turned up the volume dial on your speakers or monitor to no avail. Then you tried turning up the volume using the icon in your OS's task bar without result. There might have been middleware and hardware configurations to tinker with. Finally, you had to turn up the volume in your media player to get the results you wanted. Of course, after that you started with the media player volume only to find that this time, the speakers were the culprit. It never fails.

Pivot points are notorious for suffering from the "too-many-dials" problem (especially in Mecanim). **A pivot point, which is a single point in space, is important because it is at this point that a GameObject's transformation (translate, rotate, scale) is calculated. It is the point around which a GameObject pivots (and scales and translates).** A GameObject's pivot point problems begin at creation. When you create a mesh in an external modeling program (such as 3ds Max, Maya, or Blender), its pivot point typically defaults to the center of the object. This can be edited however and placed arbitrarily by the artist. Upon import though, Unity tends to locate the pivot point wherever it pleases, overriding the location assigned or defined in the modeling program.

In addition to different software causing pivot point conflicts, the Toolbar toggle buttons **Center/Pivot** and **Local/Global** can all override the Transformation locus. With Center active, transformations will be calculated beginning at the GameObject's center. With Pivot toggled, transformations will be calculated beginning at the GameObject's pivot point, which may or may not be the GameObject's center.

We discussed the difference between local and global coordinates in a previous chapter and here those terms exist as a toggle button. **Local makes your coordinates' system relative to a GameObject's pivot point, and global makes the GameObject's location subordinate to the world coordinates system**. What this means is that any transformations performed on a GameObject are performed on the GameObject's local coordinate system as well (as alluded to in the instance of scaling parent/child GameObjects).

So when you rotate a cube GameObject, you are also rotating its local x, y, and z coordinates. They are subjective. This is perhaps easier to understand with an example.

- Open the Scene **sec1Chap10Toolbar**.

- Select and center the Cube.

- Press W to activate the **Move Gizmo**.

- Note that the Move Gizmo's axes run parallel and perpendicular to the Scene grid.

- Select an axis of the Move Gizmo and click and drag to Translate (move) it.

- Note that it slides along at either a parallel or perpendicular angle.

- Press E to activate the **Rotate Gizmo**.

- Select the outer most orbit, click and drag to rotate the Cube.

- Note that the Z value in the Cube's Transform component changes.

- Press W to activate the **Move Gizmo**.

- Note that the cube's faces are no longer parallel and perpendicular to the Scene grid or the Move Gizmo's axes (Figure 10.6).

- Click the Toolbar's **Global** (World) toggle to switch it to **Local**.

- Note that the Move Gizmo's axes once again run parallel and perpendicular to the Scene grid; the Cube is now in a local coordinate system that treats the GameObject as its reference point.

As a practical matter, none of this needs to be worried about. Most of the time, positioning GameObjects is more of an art than science. How you go about it, World or Local, matters little. It can be frustrating, however, to select a GameObject and realize that its pivot point is nowhere to be found. Switching pivot point to Center can of course solve this, but even a step as small as this can ruin efficiencies on a long enough timeline. **Moreover, scripts and PlayMaker calculate Transformations from the pivot point. Never mind ruining efficiencies; if a pivot point is not**

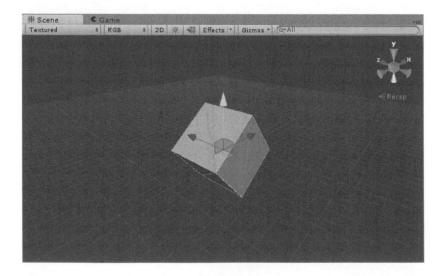

FIGURE 10.6 The changes to the Move Gizmo.

where you think it is, it can ruin the intended outcome of scripts, the PlayMaker State Machine, and ultimately the game. This begs the question, how do you define a pivot point inside Unity? You can't. There is a work-around however:

- Right-click in the Hierarchy View and select **Create Empty** from the drop-down menu.

- To rename the GameObject, select the empty GameObject and in the Inspector View type **cubePivotPoint** into the first text field.

- Select the cubePivotPoint in the Hierarchy and press W to ensure the Move Gizmo is active.

- Position the cubePivotPoint just above the Cube.

- In Hierarchy, select Cube and drag and drop it onto cubePivotPoint to create a parent/child relationship.

- Ensure the **Pivot/Center** toggle on the Toolbar is set to Pivot.

- Select cubePivotPoint, press E, and rotate.

- Note that the cube is no longer using its own pivot point and that it is using cubePivotPoint's locus instead.

- You have created an ad hoc pivot point (Figure 10.7)!

Now scripts and/or the PlayMaker State Machine can perform Transform calculations on the ad hoc pivot point's location rather than the child's potentially buggy pivot point.

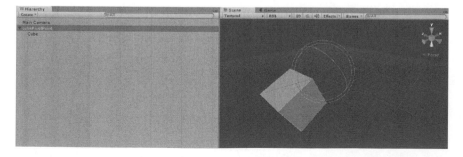

FIGURE 10.7   An ad hoc pivot point.

FIGURE 10.8   Play Mode grouping.

FIGURE 10.9   The Layers drop-down menu.

The next grouping of Toolbar Tools are the **Play Mode** buttons (Figure 10.8). Play Mode buttons control the Game View. To test your Scene by playing it, click the **Play** button. To pause the game, use the **Pause** button. To step play, use the **Step** button. To exit gameplay, click the Play button a second time. Play Mode will be discussed in greater depth along with the Game View.

At the rightmost of the Toolbar are the drop-down menus **Layers** and **Layout** (Figure 10.9). Previously, it was discussed that Layers are used to add exceptionality to GameObjects. Here, Layers can also be used for organizational purposes. To the right of each of the Layers is an eye icon and a lock icon. Both can be toggled on and off. If the eye icon is toggled closed, any GameObject belonging to that layer will be made invisible in the Scene View. Again, this is for organizational purposes and editing convenience only. The GameObjects are still active and can be seen in the Game View (and by extension, when the game is played). Toggling the lock icon has no discernible effect. Edit Layers can be accessed from this drop-down as well.

We examined the Layout submenu in a previous chapter. Layout is accessible here in the Toolbar as well. The options here are identical to those found under Window.

In Unity 5, there are a few more buttons. A cloud icon will launch Services View or, if it is already docked, switch to it. An **Account** drop-down provides yet another way to log in and out.

In this chapter, we learned all about the Toolbar. The "too-many-dials" problem and how it relates to pivot points was discussed. We performed a dirty hack that allowed us to create an ad hoc pivot point. We also learned how to translate, rotate, and scale GameObjects. By using the Layers drop-down menu, we learned how to hide GameObjects for our convenience while editing. Finally, we found an alternate way to access the Layout sub-menu. We are now going where the action is, to the Views!

CHAPTER 11

Project View

T HROUGH THE COURSE OF working with Project examples, Views have already been introduced and cursorily examined. A portion of this chapter then will be re-View.

The "Project View" is our Layout's top leftmost View (Figure 11.1). **It is a library that shows us everything that is in our Project and available to use in our game. Newly created assets first appear in the Project View. It is important to understand that any changes made to an asset are saved as part of the Project automatically (upon exit) regardless of whether or not the Scene is saved. Also, deleting an Asset deletes its Scene counterpart as well. This action is not undoable**. For example, deleting a **New Terrain** asset will permanently delete the corresponding Terrain from the Scene.

Other than processing Prefabs as described in a previous chapter, the purpose of the Project View is to store, organize, and facilitate easy access to the things you will need to put into your game. There are several fancy buttons that facilitate these functions, but the best method is to make sure you name everything in a self-descriptive manner, use a sensible folder structure, and put everything in its right place. If you can do that, you can pretty much forgo further Project View study. But before you go, know that renaming assets in the Project View can be tricky. You can select an asset and rename it in the Inspector View. This is accomplished in the Inspector View's first and topmost text input field. Note that the name might not update in Assets until the Scene has been saved.

The Project View has a bar along the top named **Project View Control Bar** (Figure 11.2). Most of the functionality here is of either the create or

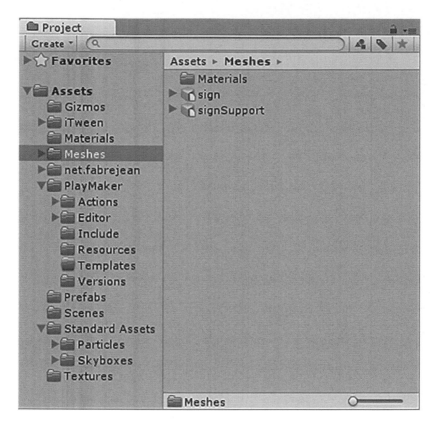

FIGURE 11.1   The Project View.

FIGURE 11.2   The Project View Control Bar.

find variety. The first option along the bar is **Create**. This is the same menu as the Create subfolder in the Assets drop-down menu. Create, and all of the options in Assets, is more easily accessed by hovering over the right-hand pane of the Project View and right-clicking. To the right of the Create button is a search field. This will allow you to search for assets by name. Note that you are not limited to searching just the assets in your scene; you can also search the Asset Store by selecting it from the drop-down menu **Search**, at the top of Project View's right-hand pane. To the right of the text input field is an icon comprised of tiny shapes: circle, square, and rectangle. Clicking on it elicits a drop-down of file types that can be used to filter search results. The next icon, a label, elicits a drop-down of **Labels**. Labels are the organizational equivalent of tags. Clicking on a label restricts search results to assets that have been assigned the selected label. Label assignment must be done manually by first selecting an asset in the Project View. In the Inspector, at the bottom, a section named **Asset Labels** will appear. Clicking the blue label icon there will allow you to assign multiple labels to an asset. Searches, and any filters (be they file type or label), can be saved by clicking on the star icon.

In the negative space just above the Project View search buttons is a lock icon and a list icon. These relate to manipulation of the Project View itself for the purposes of Layout customization. They are safely ignored as we have explored this functionality using the more intuitive methods of clicking, dragging and dropping, and docking.

At the bottom of the right-hand pane is a slider. This allows you to manipulate the folder View type. You can choose gigantic icons or dial things all the way down to a list View. The latter is recommended.

Finally, in the left-hand pane, above the Assets folder structure, is **Favorites**. Here, you can quickly search by file type. You can also drag and drop folders from the Assets folder structure into favorites to create a shortcut. Note that you can only drag and drop into Favorites from the left-hand pane. Trying to cross over from the right-hand pane, or anywhere else for that matter, will fail.

In this chapter we explored the Project View. We learned that the Project View's function is that of a library's: to store, organize, and facilitate easy access to the things you will need to put into your game. While it has many ways to help you find assets, it is simply best not to lose them in the first place. This depends on good organizational techniques such as using sensible naming conventions and proper folder management. In the next chapter, the Hierarchy View will be discussed.

CHAPTER 12

Hierarchy View

IN THIS CHAPTER, WE look briefly, very briefly, at the Hierarchy View. It is essentially a list.

Whereas the Project View stores everything that has the potential to be in our game, the "Hierarchy View" lists everything that is currently in our Scene (level) (Figure 12.1). **Newly created GameObjects appear in the Hierarchy View.** We have examined some of its abilities already; it allows for convenient selection of GameObjects and the creation of parent/child relationships. **Primarily, however, it serves as a textual list to facilitate easy GameObject selection**.

Like the Project View, the Hierarchy View comes with a Create button (Figure 12.2). This button recreates most of the GameObject drop-down menu. These and additional options are, however, more easily accessed by right-clicking in the Hierarchy View. Also, like the Project View, Hierarchy has a View panel list icon and search bar.

Unlike the Project View, folder creation is conspicuously absent. An ad hoc folder system can be created by creating an Empty GameObject and making it the parent of its intended contents. The Empty GameObject should then be renamed according to the following convention: gameobjectNameFolder. The Empty GameObject parent can be collapsed in much the same way a folder is closed to tidy up. This hack comes with a caveat however; as the parent, the Empty GameObject's transform coordinates reign supreme. **Make sure any ad hoc folder (parent) shares**

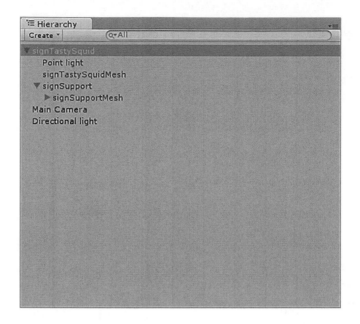

FIGURE 12.1   The hierarchy View.

FIGURE 12.2   The hierarchy View Control Bar.

the same transform values as its primary constituent (most important child). Or if doing double-duty as an ad hoc pivot point, make sure its coordinates are exactly where you want them.

This chapter, in proportion to the options provided by the Hierarchy View, was short. The Hierarchy View provides the most useful way for creating and manipulating parent/child relationships but primarily it is a selection list. Scene View is next.

CHAPTER 13

Scene View

I**N THIS CHAPTER, WE** will discuss the Scene View. We will delve into alternate modes of Scene View navigation and the most efficient mode of egress. We will also look at the different types of visual information that Scene View presents by default. Of importance are **Perspective, Isometric,** and **Orthographic** observational types and their uses.

The Scene View displays the game world in such a way as to be convenient for editing (Figure 13.1). **From the Scene View, it is easy to imagine what the level will look like when played yet it contains additional visual information and options necessary for editing. Scene View is where you position GameObjects.**

The **Scene View Control Bar** along the top offers drop-downs, buttons, and text input (Figure 13.2). The first drop-down menu offers a variety of rendering options some of which give insight into performance. **Textured** should be left as the default; this render type most resembles what the player will see. **RGB** should likewise be left as default. The button **2D Switch** is by default toggled off. Clicking it will enter 2D mode and strip the scene of its depth. Except when editing UI, it is almost never used in the creation of 3D games. The next button features a sun icon and represents the Scene's lighting. It too is toggled off by default. It may seem counterintuitive that in a new scene turning lighting *on* actually makes the Scene *go dark*. Think of the **Lighting Switch** button as representing a theater's stage lighting; toggle it on and the stage lighting takes over. Switch the stage lights off and the theater lights come up. In this analogy, that means the entire Scene editor (the theater) becomes visible. **In short,**

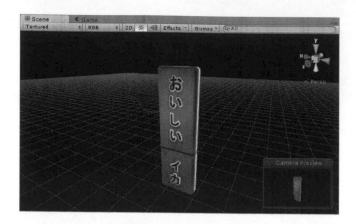

FIGURE 13.1   The Scene View.

FIGURE 13.2   The Scene View Control Bar.

having the Lighting Switch on will illuminate the Scene View with the lighting elements that you have implemented, but switching it off may make it easier to see the Scene for editing purposes. Next to Lighting Switch, the speaker icon toggles Scene sounds on and off. It is named the **Audio Switch**. The **Effects menu/button** references rendering effects such as fog. Fog is great for limiting the player's view and cultivating an atmosphere of uncertainty and dread. While that may be great for gameplay, it is awful for editing. You can turn effects such as fog on and off in the Effects menu drop-down. You can toggle Effects on and off en masse by pressing the Effects button. Note that doing so makes *absolutely no difference* as to what effects render in the Game View and resulting game; it only affects what is seen in the Scene View. The **Gizmo menu** drop-down allows you to edit what types of visual information and Gizmos are displayed in the Scene View. There shouldn't be a need to edit the Gizmo menu defaults unless you find that a Gizmo abstracts your view.

In the Scene View proper, you will see a visual representation of your Scene. It will be augmented with visual information conducive to editing. The visual information typically takes the form of icons and Gizmos. For example, the Main Camera uses an icon for representation (it lacks a mesh) and a Gizmo to illustrate its field of view. Previously, we discussed the use of the Toolbar's View Tool to navigate the Scene View. Alternative to that, holding the right mouse button down will enter you into **Flythrough** mode. You can then navigate your Scene in a manner more familiar to gamers by using the WASD keys. While in Flythrough mode, E will float you straight up, Q will move you straight down. Holding Shift will speed things up. Much of the time, however, Flythrough mode movement is unnecessary. You will want to simply teleport to whatever GameObject you have selected. This is done with hotkey F.

In the upper right-hand corner of the Scene View is the **Scene Gizmo**. First, let's define some important terms of art, literally, terms that originate from the art world.

Perspective is a type of observation that most closely resembles what we see with our eyes. It is a technique for representing 3D imagery (game world) on a 2D surface (video screen). A hallmark of perspective technique is the use of foreshortening (distorting objects as they recede) and single point convergence (parallel lines such as train tracks appear to converge in the distance). Perspective is commonly used in first-person shooters such as Call of Duty. **Isometric** view removes a sense of depth by eliminating foreshortening and single point convergence yet still supposes three dimensions. This observational type is commonly used in retro city simulation games such as SimCity. Like Isometric, **Orthographic** removes a sense of depth. The difference between Isometric and Orthographic views is that with Orthographic, the view is cast perpendicularly upon the subject. This observational type is commonly used in 2D side-scrolling games such as Super Mario Brothers (Figure 13.3).

Scene View's default observational type is Perspective. If you need an Isometric view, you can toggle the word **Persp** beneath the Scene Gizmo or by clicking the Scene Gizmo's nexus. If you want your view to align perpendicular and parallel to the world axes, you can click one of the Scene Gizmo's arms. Note that they are colored and labeled x, y, and z. Isometric + Perpendicular alignment = Orthographic.

Note that the text below the Scene Gizmo will update to keep you apprised of your orientation. If you are creating a 3D game, you will spend a lot of your time using a Perspective observational type. That being said, Orthographic vantage is much more useful for ensuring the proper positioning of GameObjects and for UI work.

Finally, Scene View has picture-in-picture functionality. With a Camera selected, a Camera Preview element will appear in the lower right-hand corner. With the Main Camera selected, the Camera Preview image is identical to the Game View image. Segue!

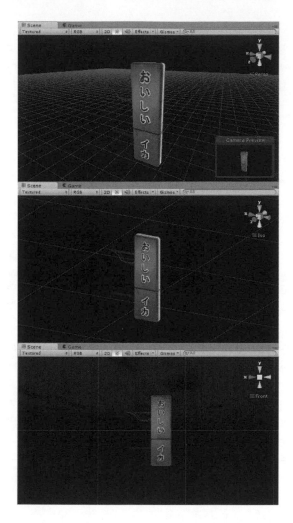

FIGURE 13.3 The differences between Perspective, Isometric, and Orthographic vantage points; note that there is no foreshortening in the Isometric or Orthographic cases.

In this chapter, we learned all about the Scene View. Scene View navigation was expanded upon. We looked at the different types of visual information contained within Scene View. We learned of the different observational types **Perspective**, **Isometric**, and **Orthographic** and their uses. In the next chapter, Game View will be discussed.

CHAPTER 14

Game View

W HAT IS IN THE **Game View** is up to you! It is the result of everything you have put into the Hierarchy View (Figure 14.1).

Game View allows you to play your game (so long as there are no game-breaking bugs). Here, you can playtest your game without having to create a build or ever leave the Unity editor. The Game View is the synergistic total of all the hard work you will put into your game creation. As mentioned earlier, it is controlled using the Play/Pause/Step buttons in the Toolbar.

The **Game View Control Bar** allows us access to the options **Aspect**, **Maximize on Play, Stats,** and **Gizmos** (Figure 14.2). The Aspect menu drop-down allows the developer to choose from several common aspect ratios. Aspect ratios describe the proportional size between a screen's width and height and have a lot in common with screen resolution. Note that forcing a particular aspect will not resize the Game View but instead creates letterbox formatting. The default, **Free Aspect,** is acceptable for daily use. Maximize on Play is another toggle button. Having it active will ensure that the Game View enlarges when the Play button is pressed. Usually, it is best to have Maximize on Play deactivated so as not to obscure the view of the Unity editor (Figure 14.3). **Stats** opens the **Rendering Statistics** overlay. The info relayed here will give valuable insight into the graphical performance of your game. Should you want the same Gizmos in your Scene View to appear in your Game View, you can edit the settings in the Gizmos drop-down menu. This is typically unwanted.

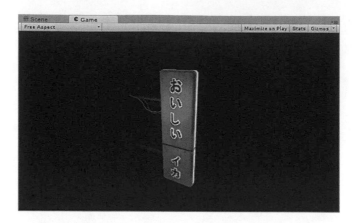

FIGURE 14.1   The Game View from the sec1Chap4Assets Scene.

FIGURE 14.2   The Game View Control Bar.

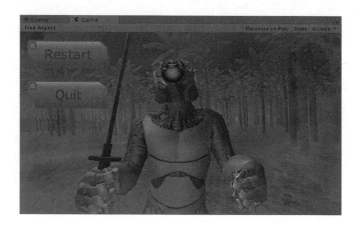

FIGURE 14.3   The final project running un-maximized in Game View.

It is possible to troubleshoot and edit your game as it runs using Unity. If not a killer, it should be considered a mortally wounding feature of Unity. The ability to edit in real time is a good reason not to activate Maximize on Play. With it deactivated, you will be able to see Unity and PlayMaker running calculations in real time. Note that when you hit Play everything but the Game View is tinted red. This is to remind you that you are in fact in Play Mode. **It is possible to make and observe changes while in Play Mode for the purposes of tweaking and troubleshooting, but the**

minute you exit Play Mode, all those changes will be lost (like tears in rain). You have been warned.

In this short chapter, we learned about the Game View and its function in playtesting. The default settings in the Game View Control Bar are ideal. Games can be edited while in Play Mode but all of the changes will be lost upon exit. Up next is the Inspector View.

CHAPTER 15

Inspector View

IN THIS CHAPTER, WE will inspect the **Inspector View**. We will review its primary and secondary purposes. In study of its primary function, we will dig into Component elements as well.

As demonstrated previously, the Inspector View is contextual (Figure 15.1). **What it displays will vary with what is selected. The Inspector View allows us insight and access to everything from assets to editor settings, but is used primarily to inspect and edit GameObject parameters and Components. With a GameObject selected, Components will appear in the Inspector View.**

When any GameObject is selected, the Inspector View will display a GameObject header (Figure 15.2). Leftmost is a cube with an arrow. Arrows of this type are used to denote that an editor element can be alternately expanded and collapsed. Clicking the cube elicits an icon menu. Here you can assign the GameObject additional visual identifiers, such as an icon, that will appear in the Scene View. Clicking the cube a second time dismisses the menu. Next to the cube is the **Activation Checkbox**. It is used to activate and deactivate the selected GameObject. It does not simply make the GameObject invisible; that would be accomplished by deactivating a **Mesh Renderer** Component. It does not destroy the GameObject; the engine can reactivate it when necessary. Deactivating a GameObject simply lets it rest inactive until such time that it requires processing resources. After the Activation Checkbox is a text input field with the GameObject's name. You can rename the GameObject here. Next is the **Static Checkbox**. Check it to inform the engine that the GameObject

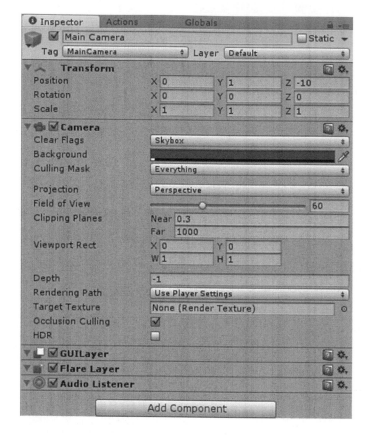

FIGURE 15.1 The Inspector View.

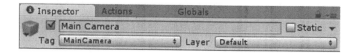

FIGURE 15.2 The Inspector View GameObject header.

is not meant to move and that it need not ever concern itself with moving the GameObject. This is done to facilitate static batching (for move on static batching refer to the Nickelcitypixels.com blog). Next to the Static Checkbox is access to a drop-down menu. Here, you can select from other optimization processes. There are a minimum of optimization techniques that even nonprogramming game developers should be aware of: object pooling, static batching, and lightmapping (aka, baking). Tags and Layers were discussed in a previous chapter. Here in the GameObject's Inspector header you can add and/or assign Tags and Layers.

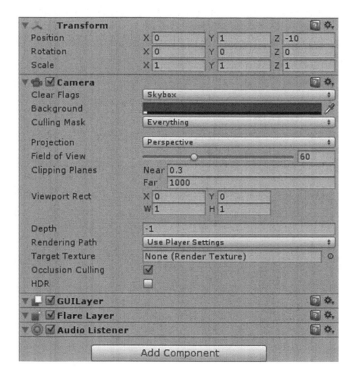

FIGURE 15.3   Elements of the Main Camera's Components.

The Inspector View allows developers to easily specify and edit a GameObject's functionality. This is done through scripts attached as Components (Figure 15.3). The first Component, and the one Component shared by all GameObjects, is the Transform Component. In the upper left-hand corner of the Component element is an arrow that can be used to collapse the Component. This saves on Inspector View real estate. With it expanded, editable variables and parameters are exposed, should there be any. In the example of the Transform Component, these parameters are Position, Rotation, and Scale values. They can be edited here and the effects can be *seen* (where else?) in the Scene View. Because the Transform Component is a prerequisite for being a GameObject, it lacks an Activation Checkbox. Other Components can be activated and deactivated which is useful when tweaking and troubleshooting. To the right of the Component's name, which is determined by the script, is a book with a question mark. This signifies **Help**. Clicking it will open up to the Component's documentation in the offline Unity Manual. The **gear** icon expands the **Component Context Menu**. This allows access to options such as **Reset, Remove**

Component, Copy/Paste Component, Move Up/Down. These options affect the Component as an element of the Inspector View.

The heart of the Inspector View is the Component, and here Components allow easy access to script variables and parameters. Values and settings can be inputted in text fields, dialed in using sliders, and selected from drop-downs.

Assets, such as materials and textures, can likewise be selected. Assets are typically chosen in a window that has been launched by clicking a target icon. Options, even the Component itself, can be toggled on and off using checkboxes. There are many ways to edit the endless expanse of Component features, most of which are typical of the visual language of software editing programs.

At the very bottom of a GameObject's Inspector View is the **Add Component** button. Here you can select Components by navigating the type hierarchy or by searching as we have done previously. You can also choose to create a **New Script** where you will be asked to name it and select a programming language. After it has been created, double-clicking it in the Project View will launch it in MonoDevelop, Unity's companion programming application. Of course, we will not be creating scripts, we will be creating PlayMaker FSMs. These too attach to a GameObject as a Component.

In this chapter, we learned that the Inspector View allows us insight and access to everything from assets to editor settings but is used primarily to inspect and edit GameObject Components. It is where GameObject meets Component, where art meets code. Here, GameObjects are given their functionality and that functionality can be further tweaked by editing the variables and parameters made available in the Component. Next is our last view, Console View.

CHAPTER 16

Console View

W E HAVE LEARNED THAT the Project View shows us everything we have available to put in game. The Scene View shows us everything we have in the current level. In this chapter, we will learn that the **Console View** shows us everything we have screwed up (Figure 16.1).

The **Console View** is like obituary for scripts. If something goes wrong with a script, you will hear about it here. The key to using the Console is to actually read the error messages. While this advice may seem laughably obvious, novice developers will often begin with the assumption that they won't understand the error messages; as a result won't even try. It is important not to be overwhelmed, to read with the intent of understanding, and to research what is unfamiliar. Remember, the purpose of error messages is to elicit solutions. **The Console View returns warning messages of varying intensity, from attention to emergency. In addition to warnings, the Console View also displays debug info and messages**. Scripts can be customized to return developer-defined messages for the purposes of troubleshooting. Double-clicking an error message will take you to the offending script.

When working with PlayMaker, you will find that the **Console View Control Bar** (Figure 16.2) defaults are preferable. These options, left to right, are **Clear, Collapse, Clear on Play, Error Pause, Open Player Log**, and **Open Editor Log**. Clear clears all messages from the Console View. Collapse eliminates repetitive messaging. Clear on Play removes all error messages upon entering Play Mode. Error Pause does *not* pause an error

FIGURE 16.1   The Console View.

FIGURE 16.2   The Console View Control Bar.

listing. Instead, when Error Pause is enabled, it will cause Play Mode to pause when an error occurs. However, Open Player Log will do just that; the information contained within will open in a text editor. Ditto for Open Editor Log.

Rightmost in the Console View Control Bar are icons representing attention, alert, and emergency error messages. Emergency level warnings must be attended to; they will prevent you from proceeding with Play Mode. They may even prevent Unity from operating. The attention, alert, and emergency buttons can be deactivated to filter out error messages of a particular type, but it is probably best not to.

Note that error messages also appear at the very bottom band of the Unity editor. It is important to acknowledge and rectify error messages.

We learned that the Console View returns error messages of varying intensity and displays debug info. We learned that to be effective, a developer must read these messages with the intent of understanding. In the next section, we will look at PlayMaker Views and the concepts and clicks that will make all our #gamedev aspirations possible.

II

All about PlayMaker

CHAPTER 17

What Is PlayMaker and What Makes It Awesome?

U NITY REVOLUTIONIZED GAME ENGINE technology. A big part of that was allowing developers to publish to multiple platforms. Among other things, this allowed users the flexibility of picking and choosing a target market (or markets) post-development as opposed to having to guess years prior. Along with digital distribution, this made game production viable for indie developers once again.

Indie development was forever changed. Indie developers, however, remained a mostly unchanged lot. While art asset sites mitigated the need for artists, a developer still needed to know how to script. It was the only way to get the engine to do what you wanted it to.

Enter PlayMaker. PlayMaker is a finite state machine framework that facilitates a highly intuitive visual scripting system. **In a finite state machine, everything exists in a state. Instructions are executed and sometimes cause a transition from one state to another**. It is a lot like real life! If you are in a sad state and someone performs the action of giving you a cupcake, you will most likely transition into a happy state. It is just about that simple! If you can create a decision tree or flowchart, you can use PlayMaker to get the engine to do what you want it to.

In addition to allowing us revolutionary development capabilities, PlayMaker gives us revolutionary troubleshooting capabilities. One of the biggest hurdles for a novice programmer is figuring out what has gone wrong when things go wrong, and things invariably go wrong. Most programming texts are mute on this point. They do little to give readers insight into the problems they are sure to encounter. With PlayMaker, troubleshooting is a simple affair. You can watch States and Transitions *highlight as they execute.* Typically the error occurs in or just before the State that never gets highlighted, never gets transitioned into! It could not be simpler, except when it is. In addition to runtime debugging, PlayMaker comes equipped with a "Realtime Error Checker (that) finds errors before you hit play."

Moreover, PlayMaker is highly extensible. Hutong games, the creators of PlayMaker, regularly update PlayMaker and augment its abilities. As does the PlayMaker Community. Many useful PlayMaker scripts are shared freely on hutonggames.com's highly active forums. If you cannot find what you need there, you may be able to find PlayMaker add-ons in the Unity Asset Store at very reasonable prices.

PlayMaker

- Allows anyone who can create a flowchart to visually script finite state machines that take the place of programming

- Allows quick and easy troubleshooting through runtime observation and Realtime Error Checking

- Like Unity, it offers free and cost-effective solutions to many problems through the public Asset Store and forums

- Allows just about anyone to develop video games

Whereas Unity redefined *indie game development*, PlayMaker redefined the *indie game developer*. The definition is no longer intrinsically linked with that of programmer; now an indie developer is anyone with the will and desire to realize their dreams! For the first time ever, game development is possible for just about anyone!

CHAPTER 18

Functions, Conditionals, Flowcharts, and Variables

Easy-Peasy Vocab

IN THIS CHAPTER, WE will learn a little about programming. I can hear readers collectively gasp and breathlessly exclaim, "but you said we weren't going to have to learn how to code! It's in the title!" Don't worry; I promise you will not have to learn the *how to*, but we will have to talk about the *how*. Our discussion will, for the most part, be limited to the vocabulary we need to know in order to operate PlayMaker. Who knows though, you may become so intrigued that you will *want* to learn how to program.

Programming is powerful. It gets its power from **variables, functions, and conditionals. A variable is storage for dynamic information. A function is one or more instructions that perform a specific task. A conditional expression decides what should be done in the event that specific information meets particular criteria such as being true or being a particular number**.

A **variable** is often likened to a container in which information is stored and from which it is retrieved. As its name implies, that information is variable, that is, it can change as the program runs. A character's health, as represented by a number from 0 to 100, would most likely be stored as an integer variable named (you guessed it) "health." The value of health (i.e., its corresponding number) will change throughout the game depending on, among other things, how many shovels the character is hit with. A **function** is comprised of one or more instructions. It is a miniprogram of sorts. A function's instructions might involve subtracting 20 from a character's "health" variable every time it got hit with a shovel. More likely, instead of 20, the function would subtract the value of the variable "damage." This way, the variable "damage" could be updated according to the kind of shovel the player is hit with. A coal shovel would do more damage than a snow shovel, which, in turn, would do more damage than one of those little plastic sand-castle shovels. A **conditional** determines what will happen as the result of new information. For example, a conditional might continuously check to see what a player's "health" is, and if it is 0 (or less), decide to play a death animation and end the game. Otherwise, it would continue to check until and unless the character meets its grizzly demise at the hands of a shovel-wielding maniac (there really should be more games where the objective is to hug your opponent).

Let's call the previous examples our CheckExistence function. It may have occurred to you that CheckExistence has all the makings of a decision tree or flowchart. That is very astute! Many programmers first diagram their program or function as a flowchart. The flowchart then serves as a blueprint from which they create their code.

The flowcharts we will be working with come in many shapes, sizes, and potentially many colors, but they will have several things in common a beginning, an end, and several pathways that will often branch in different directions. Let's recreate the CheckExistence function as a flowchart (Figure 18.1).

Note that here, as in life, there are two states: alive and dead. To make a determination between the two, we need our health variable. If we were coding we would declare, define, and assign it a value like so:

```
int health = 100;
```

Here, we have specified that the variable is going to be an integer, that is, a whole number. We have named it "health" and we have assigned it the value of 100. Let's add that to the chart (Figure 18.2).

Now we have to rephrase the "Is the player alive?" question so that the computer can understand it. Computers like it when you phrase your question in the form of a math:

```
health > 0?
```

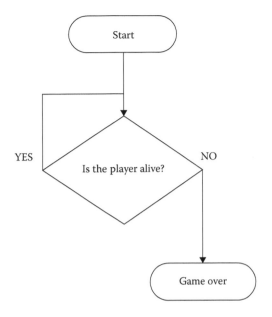

FIGURE 18.1   Our CheckExistence function as a natural language flowchart.

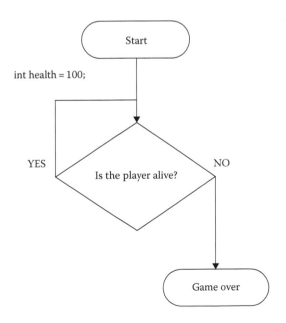

FIGURE 18.2   A variable has been added to the mix.

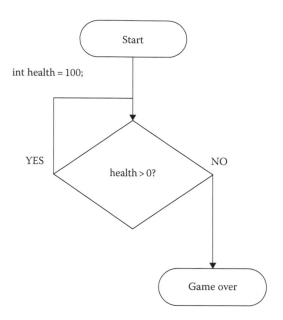

int health = 100;

FIGURE 18.3　This as close to code as we are going to get.

Remember, health is just a container for a whole number. Let's add our new, quasi-code question to the chart (Figure 18.3).

This is probably past the point at which a programmer would remake the flowchart as lines of code. Since we are using a state machine, *we will not have to*. Our flowchart *is* the code. In PlayMaker, functions will correspond to **FSMs** (finite state machines) and instructions will correspond to **Actions**. Conditionals will most closely correspond to an **Action/ Transitional Event** pair, and variables will be, well, **Variables**, which brings us back to learning code vocabulary. You will need to learn the different types of variables:

- **Integer**: Use this type when you are dealing with whole numbers.

- **Float**: Use this type when you are dealing with numbers that have decimal places.

- **Vectors 2 and 3**: Use these types when you are dealing with two or three numbers at a time. Why would you? Well to specify 2D and 3D coordinates, of course.

- **Boolean**: Use this when you want to store a true or false value for the purpose of implementing yes/no conditionals.

- **String**: Use this when you want to store text. Note that "15" stored as a string is the word 15 spelled with numbers and not the number 15.

- **Quaternion**: You shouldn't have to even worry about pronouncing this one.

There are other variables as well, which are specific to Unity and PlayMaker such as **Texture**, **Material**, and **GameObjects**. With these, you are just using your variable to keep track of which GameObject, Texture, or Material meets a certain condition. An example would be determining through a mathematical operation which GameObject with an enemy tag is the closest and then storing that information in a GameObject-typed variable named closestEnemy.

That is it for this chapter! We had a close brush with code but lived to tell the tale. We learned about functions, variables, and conditionals. We identified their PlayMaker counterparts. We also learned how to create flowcharts, and that in PlayMaker, flowcharts will *be* the code. Finally, we learned a lot of important vocabulary regarding variable types. There is a lot to learn in this chapter; it may well be worth a reread. Always remember that in a finite state machine, everything exists in a state. Instructions are given and sometimes the instruction results cause a transition from one state to another. The next chapter begins a new section, PlayMaker.

CHAPTER 19

PlayMaker View

I N THIS CHAPTER, WE will look at the PlayMaker View. It is important to know the information contained herein but do not be frustrated if it seems abstract; learning will come by way of doing in succeeding chapters. In fact, it is a good idea to learn the PlayMaker View section names and then skip the rest of the chapter. Refer back when the need arises; this chapter is primarily reference.

The PlayMaker View is comprised of the following sections (Figure 19.1):

1. **Selection Toolbar**

2. **PlayMaker Graph View**

3. **Inspector Panel (complete with Control Bar)**

4. **Debug Toolbar**

5. **Preferences**

The Selection Toolbar enables the survey and selection of finite state machines (FSMs). In the PlayMaker Graph View, the state machine's States are mapped out and linked together with Transitional Events. The Inspector Panel allows for the configuration of the FSM, the creation and specification of Events, and the definition, declaration, and value assignment of Variables. In addition to PlayMaker View, we have docked the PlayMaker Actions, Ecosystem, and Globals Views. Actions View allows for the search and selection of the Actions (instructions)

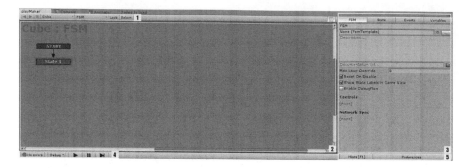

FIGURE 19.1 The PlayMaker View with a newly created FSM attached to a Cube GameObject (sections to be detailed individually).

FIGURE 19.2 The Selection Toolbar as it appears across the top of the PlayMaker View.

that power the state machine. Ecosystem enables the user to search, download, and install add-on Packages for PlayMaker. Moreover, the Packages and Actions are often accompanied by links to documentation and tutorials. The Globals View is similar to the Variables tab in the Inspector Panel except that it provides for the creation of Global Variables, variables that are accessible from any FSM.

Across the top of the PlayMaker View is the Selection Toolbar (Figure 19.2). It allows the user to survey and select from the FSMs in the Scene. The left and right arrows allow you to cycle forward and backward through the most recently visited FSMs. Adjacent is the list icon **Recent**. It elicits a drop-down selection of recently visited FSMs and their GameObject pairing. It also identifies any Prefab from which these parts are derived. The **Select GameObject** drop-down shows all the GameObjects that have an FSM attached to them. Conversely, the following **Select FSM** drop-down allows you to see and select all the FSMs that are attached to the currently selected GameObject. **Of all the Selection Toolbar buttons, the Select FSM button is the most useful. It is common to lose track of all the attached FSMs, and there is no alternate access point for multiple attached FSMs in PlayMaker View**. The **Lock** button locks PlayMaker View's display of the currently enabled FSM regardless of anything else being selected. The final drop-down menu, when applicable, allows you to toggle between the Prefab and Prefab Instance or, if the Prefab is selected, to

FIGURE 19.3   The Graph View.

create an instantiation. Alternately, it allows you to select the GameObject to which the FSM is attached. The final button allows you to turn off or on the **Graph View Mini-Map**.

Strictly speaking, the Graph View (Figure 19.3) is not a true View; it cannot be separated from PlayMaker View nor can it be docked or independently resized. Its purpose is to map out the state machine and puts the visual in visual scripting. **After selecting a GameObject, an FSM can be attached to it by right-clicking anywhere in the Graph View and clicking on Add FSM in the resulting menu. Note that adding an FSM adds the PlayMaker FSM (Script) to the GameObject as a Component. It can be viewed and partially edited in the Inspector View. Variables that have been marked as exposed to the Inspector can be observed in the Inspector View as well**. With an FSM established, right-clicking the Graph View's negative space subsequently elicits a larger menu of options (Figure 19.4).

FIGURE 19.4   The Graph View's FSM right-click menu.

- **Add State** will create a new State.

- **Paste State** will paste a copied State(s) into Graph View.

- **Paste Template** will paste a Template into Graph View.

- **Copy FSM** will copy the current FSM to clipboard.

- **Save Template** allows you to save the current FSM as a Template that you can reuse by insertion into other FSMs.

- **Set Watermark** opens a set of Watermark Textures that allows you to add a watermark to the Graph View that visually distinguishes the FSM.

- **Save Screenshot** copies an already cropped image of Graph View's state machine to your OS's clipboard.

- **Add FSM Component** opens a submenu from which you can add a **New FSM**, **Paste FSM**, or **Add Template** to the GameObject.

- **Remove FSM Component** deletes the FSM and removes the corresponding Component from the GameObject.

In creating an FSM, a **Start Event** and **State 1** State are created as well. Right-clicking the State evokes a menu (Figure 19.5).

- **Add Transition** allows you to choose from the ubiquitous **FINISHED** Transition, any **Custom Events**, and the **System Events** and **Network Events** submenus.

- **Add Global Transition** allows you to choose from global versions of the preceding Transitions.

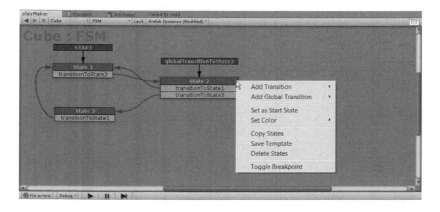

FIGURE 19.5   State's right-click menu.

- **Set as Start State** allows you to simultaneously eliminate the default Start State and assign it to the selected State.

- **Set Color** enables the user to color code selected States.

- **Copy States** copies States.

- **Save Template** saves the State as a Template.

- **Delete States** allows you to delete the selected State(s).

- **Toggle Breakpoint** allows you to turn a State's pause functionality on (or off) before its Actions execute in order to facilitate runtime debugging.

To facilitate movement from one state to another, a Transition is added to a State. With added Transitions come additional right-click menus (Figure 19.6).

- **Sent By... is a very useful menu option that will tell you which, if any, other FSMs trigger the Transition (provided it is Global)** *and* **which State it is sent from**.

- **Transition Event** enables the specification of the currently selected Transition as either the ubiquitous FINISHED Event, a Custom Event, or an Event from the System Events and Network Events submenus.

- **Transition Target** allows you to choose a State from a submenu and link to it (it is easier to do this manually).

- **Link Style** allows you to stylize the Graph View arrows as either Bezier or Circuit.

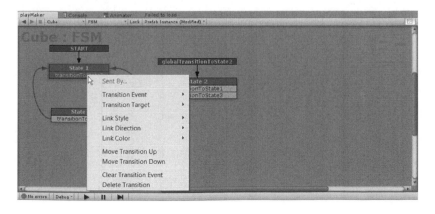

FIGURE 19.6   A Transition's right-click menu.

- **Link Style Direction** allows you to choose Left or Right directions for the Graph View arrows.

- **Link Color** enables the user to color code selected Links.

- **Move Transition Up** moves the Transition higher in a list containing multiple Transitions.

- **Move Transition Down** moves the Transition lower in a list containing Transitions.

- **Clear Transition Event** vacates the Transition of its specification without removing the Transition from the State.

- **Delete Transition** removes the Transition from the State.

To facilitate communication between two or more FSMs, a Global Transition is added to a State. With added Global Transitions come (you guessed it) additional right-click menus (Figure 19.7).

Global Transition's right-click menu is simply a truncated Transition right-click menu. The options and their effects are the same.

Along the top of the PlayMaker View, Inspector Panel is a series of buttons that is not unlike Control Bars elsewhere in Unity (Figure 19.8). For that reason, it is referred throughout the book as a Control Bar. The Control

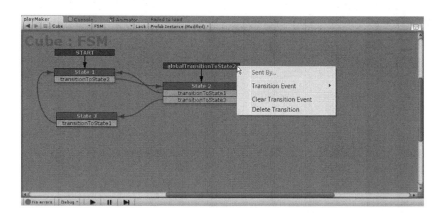

FIGURE 19.7 A Global Transition's right-click menu.

FIGURE 19.8 The Inspector Panel Control Bar.

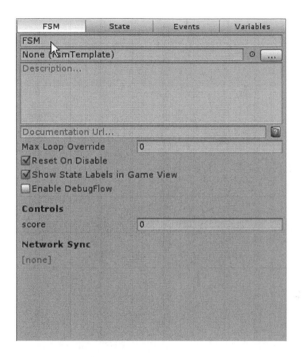

FIGURE 19.9   The FSM Inspector.

Bar buttons allow you to inspect the selected FSM, State, all locally created local and global Events, and all local Variables.

The FSM Inspector is used primarily to edit the FSM's name and description (Figure 19.9). FSM inspection can also be achieved through the FSM Component in Unity's Inspection View. The first field allows editing of the FSM's name. Changes to the name will update throughout the PlayMaker View, for example, in the selection lists of the Selection Toolbar and in the Graph View. The second row allows the developer to select an FSM Template. The largest field enables editing of the FSM's description. Edits made here will update in the FSM Component and in the Graph View. Should the FSM require additional explanation and documentation, the developer should post it online. The documentation's URL should then be entered into the field beneath the FSM's description.

- **Max Loop Override** allows you to override the maximum loop count (but don't).

- **Reset on Disable**, if unchecked, allows the user to pause an FSM by disabling the corresponding Component in Inspector View.

- **Show State Labels in Game View** allows you to see which GameObjects have FSMs as the game plays. This setting can be overridden in Preferences in the parameter of the same name. There it is necessary to disable the display of State Labels before creating a build from the Project.

- **Enable DebugFlow** is deactivated by default for performance reasons, otherwise DebugFlow records variables and State information as the game plays.

- **Controls** takes any variables marked for exposure and exposes them in the Inspector View for the purposes of runtime debugging (troubleshooting while the game runs).

- **Network Sync** takes any variables marked for Network Sync and exposes them in the Inspector View.

When working in PlayMaker View, most of the developer's time will be equally divided between Graph View and the State Inspector, with the remainder of the time spent searching Actions and creating Events and Variables. With State active in the Inspector Panel Control Bar, the developer can add and edit the Actions of the selected State (Figure 19.10).

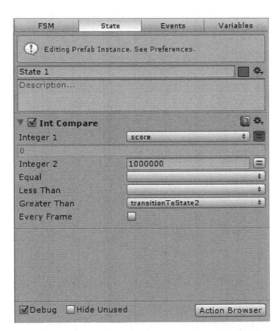

FIGURE 19.10   Inspection of the currently selected State.

Accordingly, what is gleaned from State Inspection is very much dependent upon what Actions the developer adds to the State. There are some constants though. If, for example, an Instance is being edited rather than the Prefab (should either exist), a warning will appear. Otherwise, the first element is the **State Name** field where the State's name is assigned. Edits will update the selected State in Graph View. To the right of the State's name field is a square icon that facilitates the application of color to the State's Graph View header. The cog wheel icon opens the **Settings Menu** which grants the user the ability to toggle certain settings for State Inspection. The defaults are suitable. Additionally, the menu allows for the manipulation of Actions. Most of these options are self-explanatory, redundant, and more easily accessible elsewhere however.

- **Debug** exposes the values of variables.

- **Hide Unused** prunes Action Editor parameter fields that are both optional and unspecified.

- The **Action Browser** button launches the Action Browser View (aka Actions View).

Adding an Action from the **Action Browser** adds an **Action Editor** to the State (Figure 19.11). What appears in the Action Editor is largely dependent upon the Action. Again, there are some constants. Note that the PlayMaker Action Editor borrows iconography from the Unity Component. The first, largest triangle allows the user to collapse/expand the Action Editor. The checkbox allows the user to **Enable/Disable** the Action (useful for testing purposes). Adjacent is the Action's **Name**. The book/question mark icon, of course, links to **Help**, online. Following is the **Settings Menu** icon. The Settings Menu options are self-explanatory and the defaults sufficient.

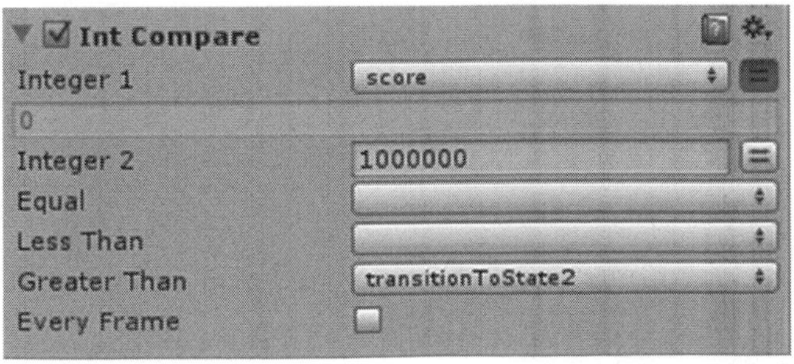

FIGURE 19.11   The Action Editor of the Int Compare Action.

The body of the Action Editor is comprised of **Action Parameters**. In the example, **Int Compare**, the first Parameter is **Integer 1**. Rightmost of this row is the **Variable/Parameter Toggle**. If it is disengaged, a field will be made available into which you can type an unchanging value. If the Toggle is engaged, the field becomes a drop-down menu from which you can select a variable (provided, of course, you have first created a variable in the Variables Manager). In Figure 19.11, the Toggle is engaged and the variable **score** has been selected. Not pictured is the **Browse Button**, that is, a square icon containing up/down arrows. This typically accompanies a text editable field and allows the alternate option of selecting from a menu. Similarly, field-length bars with up/down arrow iconography elicit a drop-down menu. Because Action Int Compare is a conditional, it requires the user to select a Transition Event using the previous menu type. In the Greater Than parameter, **transitionToState2** has been selected.

The **Events Manager** is used primarily to create and edit Events (Figure 19.12). **Note that the term "Event" is short for "Transitional Event." In the Graph View, Transitional Events are referred to as Transitions, and in the Event Manager, Transitional Events are referred**

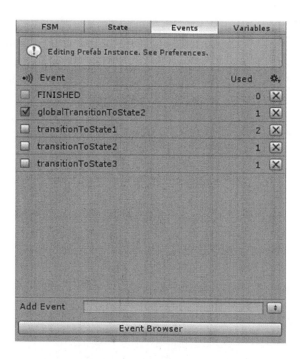

FIGURE 19.12 The Events Manager.

to as Events, but they are the same thing. The first row lists **Event, Used**, and the **Settings Menu**. The column beneath Event are Event names and the column beneath Used is a counter that displays the number of times the particular Event has been used. The **Settings Menu** opens to reveal **Remove Unused Events, Event Browser**, and **Online Help**. Remove Unused Events and Online Help are self-explanatory; the Event Browser (aka Events View) enables access to premade Events and all currently used Events.

To create a **Custom Event**, enter a name into the Add Event field toward the bottom of the Events Manager and hit enter. The Custom Event will begin, or be added to, a list of Custom Events. To the very left of the newly created Custom Event, an unchecked checkbox will appear. **Checking the box will set the Event as Global, meaning that it can be accessed from any FSM in the Scene. This is very useful as it enables the interconnectedness of FSMs, allowing them to send and receive instructions to each other**. At the opposite end of the Custom Event is a box with an X. Clicking this icon will remove the Event from the list. Existing Events can be added to the list by clicking the up/down arrows icon in the Add Event row. Underneath that is the Event Browser button, which acts as yet another access point for the Events View (Figure 19.13).

Premade Events whose names are in all caps serve as both Action and Transitional Event all-in-one. They fit into one of two categories: System Events and Global Events. Using these can improve the efficiency

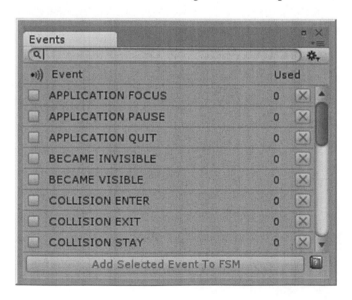

FIGURE 19.13   The Events View.

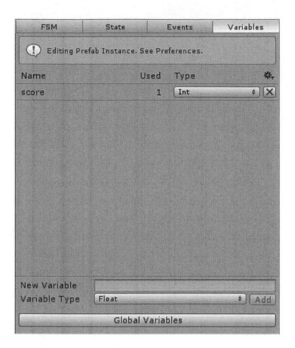

FIGURE 19.14   The Variables Manager.

of development. Particularly useful System Events include **FINISHED, ON-CLICK, COLLISION, TRIGGER**, and **KEY** and **MOUSE**–related Events. The Events View itself, however, is not particularly useful; it is made redundant by the accessibility provided by right-clicking a State in the Graph View.

The **Variables Manager** is used primarily to declare, define, and assign variables (Figure 19.14). The first row displays the text **Name, Used, Type**, and the icon for the **Settings Menu**. The Settings Menu's functionality and defaults are mostly self-explanatory. **Debug Variable Values** exposes the values of the variables in the Variables Manager. It may be worthwhile enabling this setting. **Global Variables** will launch the Global Variables Window (aka Globals View). It is recommended that Globals View be docked to the right of the Actions View.

To create a new variable, enter a name into the **New Variable** field toward the bottom of the Variables Manager. Choose the variable type and click the **Add** button. Note that the lower portion of the Variables Manager changes from facilitation of variable creation to variable editing. This change happens automatically after creating a new variable; it can be triggered manually by selecting a variable for editing (Figure 19.15).

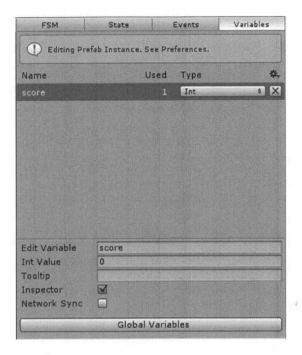

FIGURE 19.15   Variables Manager transformed to facilitate editing.

- **Edit Variable** allows you to change the name of the selected variable.

- * **Value** allows you to assign a default value to the selected variable (e.g., assign 100 to a health variable).

- **Tooltip** allows you to add descriptive text to the variable that will be visible when hovering over the variable name in the Inspector View (provided the variable is marked for Inspector View exposure).

- **Inspector**, when checked, exposes the variable in the Inspector View. **It is recommended that you *always* expose variables in the Inspector View as it is integral to runtime troubleshooting**.

- **Network Sync** syncs the selected variable throughout the network. Its functionality depends upon having a properly configured NetworkView component in the Scene.

Once added, the new variable will begin, or be added to, a list. It will occupy a row that will display its name, the number of times it is used throughout the FSM, its type (which can be selected and redefined), and a removal button. To create a new variable requires deselecting any

FIGURE 19.16   The Debug Toolbar.

presently selected variables by clicking in the Manager's negative space. **Note that the variables in the Variables Manager are local, which means that they are intended for use only by the FSM in which they are created. Create variables for use by multiple FSMs in the Globals View.** The **Global Variables** button at the bottom of the Variables Manager provides an additional access point for the Global Variables Browser (aka Globals View).

At the bottom of the PlayMaker View is the Debug Toolbar (Figure 19.16). Left to right, the Debug Toolbar sections are the **Error Count/Error Checker Window** (aka Error Check View) launch button, **Debug Menu**, and **Play Controls**.

- **Error Count/Error Checker Window** button displays how many things have gone wrong. It also functions as a button to launch Error Check View, which gives important information about where and what things have gone wrong.

- **Debug Menu** opens a menu allowing the user to tailor debug settings.

- **Play Controls** both controls Play Mode and displays any status effects; for example, if an error occurs, an error icon will appear.

Not pictured are **Prev** and **Next** buttons that are made available by enabling Debug Flow in Preferences. These allow you to either fast forward or rewind the game's time until the now temporal point exists in either the next or previous State, respectively. Note that during this process, you can select other FSMs to identify what is happening concurrently. Alternately, you can **Open Log** to make that determination.

The final PlayMaker View constituent is **Preferences** (Figure 19.17). Located beneath the Inspector Panel, Preferences is comprised of **Hints** and Preferences. Hints is a button that toggles advice for novice developers on and off. It can be useful when first learning PlayMaker but will quickly get in the way.

FIGURE 19.17   Preferences.

FIGURE 19.18 Preferences active in the Inspector Panel.

Engaging the Preferences button will allow the user to customize the PlayMaker editor in the Inspector Panel (Figure 19.18). Configurable sections include **General**, **Graph View**, **Error Checking**, and **Debugging** and are selectable from the topmost drop-down menu. The editable editor parameters are named descriptively. The defaults, by and large, are satisfactory. Once again, it will be necessary to disable Show State Labels in Game View before building, however.

In this chapter, we took an exhausting but nonexhaustive look at PlayMaker View and its many settings and functions. In the next chapter, we will look at the Action, Globals, and Ecosystem Views.

CHAPTER 20

Additional Views

I**N CHAPTER** 19, **WE** covered at the PlayMaker View. In this chapter we will look at the remaining Views that we added to the custom playMakerLayout. Much like the last chapter, this chapter is intended as reference. Those who learn better by doing are encouraged to skip ahead.

The Actions View (aka Action Browser) provides you with the Actions (instructions) that fuel your finite state machine creations (Figure 20.1). **In short, Actions do stuff**. In the Actions View, the user is furnished two ways to find a desired Action. The first is a **Search Bar**. Like most of the Unity and PlayMaker, Actions are named self-descriptively. As a result, Action names often double as keywords. If, for example, you were looking to compare two integers, you would enter the search term "integers compare" or "compare integers." As you typed, the long list of Actions would be pared away, eliminating from the list any Action that didn't strictly meet the criteria as spelled out. In this way, you might come upon the Action **Int Compare**.

The second way of finding a desired Action is to click on one of the field-length **Action Category** buttons. Doing so expands the Category to reveal its constituents. If, for example, you typed fast enough, you might eliminate Int Compare from the search results as a consequence of typing "integer" in its entirety. Int Compare could then be discovered by expanding the Action Category of **Logic** (the most commonly used types of variables are manipulated using **Math** and Logic Actions). It is a good practice to familiarize yourself with and study the different types of Actions and Action Categories early on.

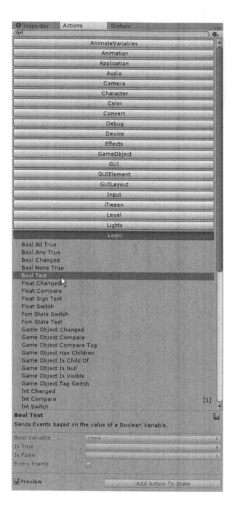

FIGURE 20.1   The Actions View.

With an Action selected and the **Preview** box checked, a ghostly pre-view appears at the bottom of the Actions View. It reveals what the Action will look like when added to a State. Additionally, there appears a helpful description and a Help icon just above the preview. It is recommended that you dedicate some time to the study of the Actions' descriptions. This way you will know what you need when the need arises.

At the top of the Actions View is a **Settings Menu** icon. At the bottom of the View is a button labeled **Add Action To State** although this is more easily accomplished by simply double-clicking the Action's name. Finally, listed Actions display the number of times they have been added to States. This number is displayed in the same row as the Action's name.

The Globals View (aka Global Variables) needs no explanation (Figure 20.2). It is a near carbon copy of the Variables Manager except that it serves Global Variables. Global Variables are variables that can be accessed from any FSM.

Ecosystem is PlayMaker's Actions and Packages manager (Figure 20.3). It empowers the developer to find and download additional, task-specific Actions (such as Animator and UI Proxies) and Templates. In many instances, search results will also return documentation, even video tutorials.

FIGURE 20.2   The Globals View.

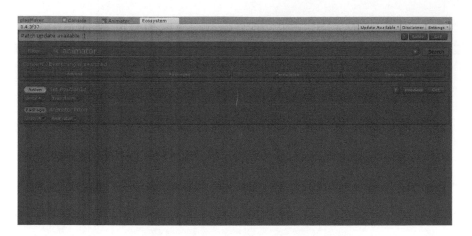

FIGURE 20.3   Ecosystem View with the Filter option activated.

After loading Ecosystem and selecting **Use Ecosystem** during its first run, its typical interface displays (alternately, it may prompt you to upgrade PlayMaker). Along the top, left to right, Ecosystem will remind you of your Unity version, inform you if there is an **Update Available**, offer a **disclaimer**, and provide a **Settings Menu**. As is usual, the default settings are both self-explanatory and self-satisfactory. Should a patch be available, Ecosystem will chide you in the second row from the top. Links to a Change Log, a **Later** button for temporary message dismissal and a **Get** (patch update) button are provided. The third row includes a **Filter** button, the **Search Bar**, and the **Search** button. Its use will be immediately apparent to anyone who has ever used a web browser. Activation of the Filter button will elicit additional buttons: **Actions**, **Packages**, **Templates**, and **Samples**. Activating a button will restrict subsequent searches to the button's proclaimed type.

Search results return below. Results in green indicate that the Actions are already installed. A result lists its type (e.g., Action, Package), its name, and its keywords. Hovering over a result summons additional buttons: **?**, **Preview**, and **Get**. The question mark button serves to display links to the result's documentation, if any, at the bottom of the Ecosystem View. The Preview button links to the resulting code's online repository. The final button, Get, downloads and imports the selected search result. Thus, the Project's Action Inventory expands and its potential increases.

In this chapter, we examined the remaining Views facilitating state machine construction. In the next chapter, we will implement our accumulated knowledge and create a Project and a Scene.

CHAPTER 21

Recreating CheckExistence as a Finite State Machine

I N CHAPTER 18, WE learned that drawing a flowchart is often done before writing code. We also learned that in PlayMaker, the flowchart *is* the code. In this chapter, we will recreate the CheckExistence flowchart as an FSM.

If you skipped the previous two chapters, here are some tips to be aware of even though they are not immediately relevant:

1. **Along the Selection Toolbar (at the top of PlayMaker View), the Select FSM drop-down (fifth option from the left) allows you to select from multiple FSMs attached to the same GameObject (and is the only access point for these FSMs in PlayMaker View).**

2. **To see what other FSM sends a message *into* a Global Transition, right-click the Global Transition and select Sent By....**

3. **Enabling Debug Flow allows you to manually step through States as well as see what is happening concurrently in other FSMs (useful for troubleshooting).**

4. **You can remove State Labels from Game View by unchecking Show State Labels in Game View in Preferences.**

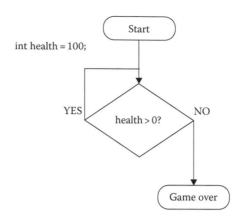

FIGURE 21.1   The final form of our CheckExistence function's flowchart.

Before we recreate the flowchart, let's reacquaint ourselves with it. The CheckExistence flowchart represented a function of the same name that checked to see which state of existence an object was in: an **alive** state or a **dead** state. The determination was made by comparing its **health** variable, an integer, to the number 0. If health was greater than 0, it was *alive* and instructions were given to repeat the check. If health was less than 0, it was *dead* and transitioned into a **game over** state (Figure 21.1).

Let's begin by creating and preparing our Scene and Project. Accomplish the following steps:

- Create a Project named **section2**.

- Import PlayMaker.

- If it is not the default, load the PlayMakerLayout.wlt Custom Layout.

- Right-click the negative space in **Project View Assets** and select **Create>Folder**.

- Name the folder **Scenes**.

- Choose **Select File>Save Scene as…**.

- Save the scene as **sec2Chap21RecreatingCheckExistencePractice** in the newly created Scenes folder (Figure 21.2).

- Download and import **section2.unitypackage** for reference.

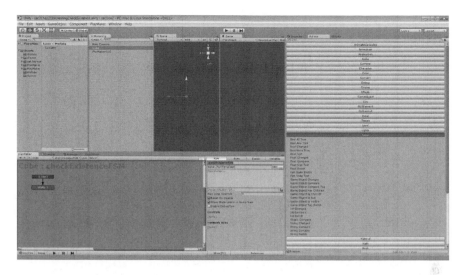

FIGURE 21.2   The Scene thus far.

Great! Let's see how PlayMaker works. Begin recreating CheckExistence by doing the following:

- In the **Hierarchy View**, right-click and select **3D Object>Cube**.

- Select **Cube** and in **PlayMaker View's** Graph View, right-click and **Add FSM** (Figure 21.3).

- With **FSM** activated in the Inspector Panel Control Bar, rename the FSM as **checkExistenceFSM**.

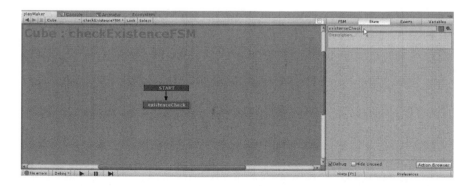

FIGURE 21.3   The PlayMaker View thus far.

- Reposition the state machine into the center of the Graph View by clicking, holding, and dragging **State 1**.

- Rename State 1 as **existenceCheck** in the State Inspector.

- Right-click in the Graph View and **Add State**.

- Rename the State **alive**.

- Position alive to the right of existenceCheck.

- Right-click in the Graph View and Add State.

- Rename the State **dead**.

- Position dead to the left of existenceCheck (Figure 21.4).

- With **Events** activated in the Control Bar, **Add Event** "**toAlive**" (and press Enter).

- Add Event **toDead** (and press Enter) (Figure 21.5).

Remember that in the Inspector Panel, "Transitional Event" is shortened to "Event," and in Graph View, "Transitional Event" is shortened to "Transition." Therefore, "Event" and "Transition" are essentially the same thing.

- In Graph View, Right-click **existenceCheck** and select **Add Transition>toAlive**.

- Right-click existenceCheck and select **Add Transition>toDead**.

- Click on Transition **toAlive** and drag a Link arrow to State **alive**.

- Click on Transition **toDead** and drag a Link arrow to State **dead** (Figure 21.6).

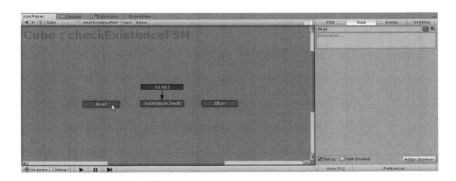

FIGURE 21.4   The PlayMaker View thus far.

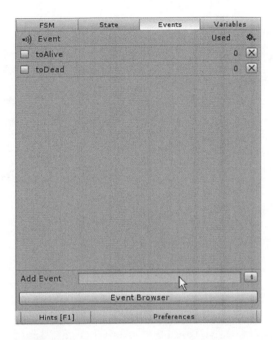

FIGURE 21.5   The Manager.

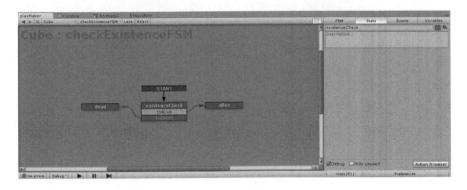

FIGURE 21.6   The PlayMaker View thus far.

The dead State is a dead end, quite literally. We do not want the alive State to end however. If the Cube is still alive, we want to still be checking. We will use a FINISHED Transition to loop back into the CheckExistence State.

- Right-click State **alive** and select **Add Transition>FINISHED**.

- Click on Transition **FINISHED** and drag a Link arrow to State **existenceCheck**.

- Click on State **dead**.

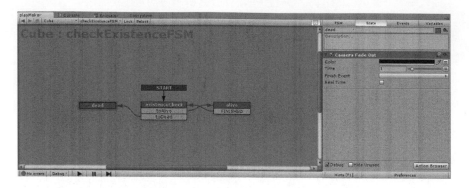

FIGURE 21.7   The PlayMaker View thus far.

- In Actions View, search **fade out**.

- Double-click the remaining result, **Camera Fade Out** (Figure 21.7).

- The Action Camera Fade Out has been added to the dead State.

Our existenceCheckFSM resembles our CheckExistence flowchart. We have a start State, a conditional State, a Transition that loops back into the conditional State, and a Transition that leads into a dead end. Unlike the flowchart, our finite state machine lacks a variable (health) and a conditional statement (health > 0?). Let's create the variable.

- Activate **Variables** in the Control Bar.

- In the Variables Manager, type **health** into the **New Variable** field.

- In the **Variable Type** row, click the **Float** rollout and select **Int**.

- Click **Add**.

- Note that the create New Variable dialogue becomes an **Edit Variable** dialogue.

- Type **100** into the **Int Value** field (and press Enter).

- Check the box next to **Inspector** by clicking it (Figure 21.8).

We now have the variable created. We still need to create the equivalent of a conditional statement. In the flowchart, we phrased the conditional as "health > 0?" Always keep in mind that a variable is just a container and not what it contains. In this case, our health variable contains an integer

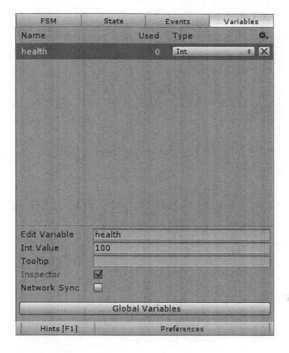

FIGURE 21.8   The Variables Manager.

(currently 100) that we are comparing to another integer, 0. For our FSM, we will need an Action that compares two integers.

- Click on State **existenceCheck**.

- In **Actions View**, clear the search bar and then search **compare**.

- Double-click the desired result, **Int Compare**.

- The **Action** Int Compare has been added to the existenceCheck **State**.

- In the **State Inspector**, click on the **Variable Toggle** in the **Integer 1** row (Figure 21.9).

- From the resulting **None** rollout, select health.

- In the **Equal** row rollout, select **toDead**.

- In the **Less Than** row rollout, select toDead.

- In the **Greater Than** row rollout, select **toAlive**.

- Check the box next to **Every Frame** by clicking it (Figure 21.10).

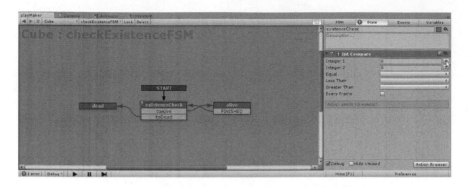

FIGURE 21.9   The resulting PlayMaker View with the cursor arrow poised over the State Inspector's Integer 1 Variable Toggle.

FIGURE 21.10   A configured Int Compare Action as it appears in the State Inspector.

We have created an FSM! Let's review what we have done. We have a GameObject, Cube, and we want to determine if it is alive or dead. We created an FSM for Cube that is comprised of States, Actions, and Transitional Events. We also created a variable: health. With health, we can determine Cube's state of existence. In the first State, the existenceCheck, we compare

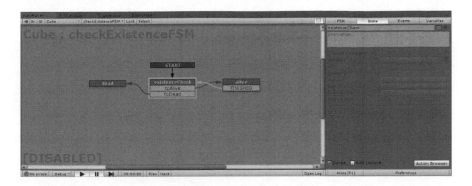

FIGURE 21.11 Nonworking FSM.

health to the number 0. If health is equal to or less than 0, we transition into State dead, where we instruct the camera to fade to black. If health is greater than 0, great! The game can continue. We transition into State alive and then back into existenceCheck. So long as Cube does not die, we continue checking on its health. Let's test our new FSM (prepare to be disappointed) (Figure 21.11).

- Hit the Play button.

- Note that the FSM is not working; it is **DISABLED**.

- Hit the Pause button.

21.1 TROUBLESHOOTING

Despite the fact that the Debug Toolbar returns **No errors**, something has gone so critically wrong that the FSM was forced **DISABLED**. Unity's Console prints out a message just beneath PlayMaker View's Debug Toolbar: **Cube: checkExistenceFSM: Loop count exceeded maximum: 1000 Default is 1000. Override in FSM Inspector**. While overriding the default loop limit in the FSM Inspector is bad advice, the message (and Graph View) provides us with valuable insight. What the message is saying is that the state machine is looping too many times; it is simply going around and around and around tying up and wasting resources. In Graph View, we can see where it is looping by observing that the FINISHED Link is highlighted. We are able to deduce that the FSM is looping between the existenceCheck and alive States too many times.

While having an alive State may make sense from a right-brained perspective (it balances the FSM visually and is aesthetically pleasing), it does not make much sense logically. After all, nothing actually happens in the alive State. A developer's first instinct should be to eliminate anything extraneous. Let's get rid of it.

- Hit Play to exit Play Mode.

- Right-click the alive State and select **Delete States**.

- Note that a red exclamation point appears; that is because Transition toAlive no longer leads anywhere.

It may be tempting to click toAlive and drag a link back into existence-Check. It is possible to do so and would most resemble our flowchart. Doing so would elicit the same error as before however. That is because Transitioning from toAlive into existenceCheck is redundant; we have already instructed the State to loop by checking **Every Frame** in the Int Compare action. This ensures that the integer in health and the integer 0 are compared each and every frame that the game runs, thereby taking the place of a link-facilitated loop. Every Frame checkboxes are a typical wellspring of errors for novice PlayMaker developers. In this instance, however, we will want to get rid of the toAlive transition.

- Right-click the **toAlive** State and select **Delete Transition**.

- Select **existenceCheck** and in the State Inspector, set **Greater Than** to **None**.

- Hit **Play**.

- Congratulations! No errors.

- Hit Play again to exit Play Mode.

That is it! We successfully recreated our flowchart as a functioning FSM. Of course, our Cube is currently immortal because there is nothing that can subtract from the health variable (there are not any shovel-wielding maniacs). Nonetheless, it is a start and unlocks the achievement: Beginner Game Developer! In the next chapter we will create a sample Scene.

CHAPTER 22

PlayMaker Sample Scene

T HERE ARE SOME ACTIONS whose usage constantly reoccurs. Their common occurrence is a reflection of their usefulness. We will implement some of these useful, ubiquitous Actions in a PlayMaker Sample Scene.

Some Actions you will use time and time again. Actions such as Move To/Towards, Look At/Smooth Look At, Activate GameObject, Get/Set Position, Raycast, and Actions in the Logic and Math categories are as capable as they are common. These Actions often provide the foundation for a game's functionality. Additionally, the importance and use of Empty GameObjects, parenting, materials, and variables will be imparted. This Scene will be comprised of a patrolling enemy, a placeable turret, and a homing missile. Let's begin with the creation of our patrolling enemy.

- Select **File>New Scene**.

- **Select File>Save Scene as....**

- Save the scene as **sec2Chap22PlayMakerSampleScenePractice** in the **Scenes** folder.

- In the Hierarchy View right-click and select **Light>Directional Light**.

- In the Hierarchy View right-click and select **3D Object>Terrain**.

- With **Terrain** selected, in the Inspector View, ensure that its **Transform** Component's **Position** coordinates are **0, 0, 0**.

- In the **Terrain (Script)** Component, click the cogwheel icon (Settings Menu).

- Under heading **Resolution**, set both **Terrain Width** and **Terrain Length** to 20 (Figure 22.1).

- In Scene View, adjust your point of observation so that you can see nearly all of the Terrain from an oblique angle.

- Select **Main Camera** from the Hierarchy View list.

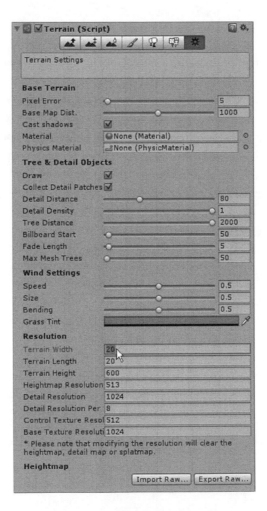

FIGURE 22.1   An illustration of the edited parameters.

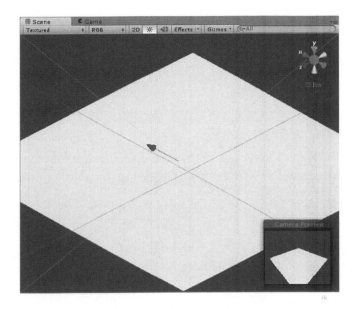

FIGURE 22.2   Main Camera that has been properly aligned with the Scene View's observation point.

- Press Ctrl+Shift+F to align Main Camera with your Scene View's observation point (Figure 22.2).

- In the Hierarchy View, right-click and select **Create Empty**.

- In the Inspector View, rename **GameObject** to **pointA**.

- With pointA selected, in the Inspector View, ensure that its **Transform** Component's **Position** coordinates are **10, 1, 1**.

- Reselect pointA in the Hierarchy View and press Ctrl+D to duplicate it.

- In the Inspector View, rename pointA to **pointB**.

- In the Scene View, reposition pointB so that its Z value is approximately **12**.

We now have the waypoints that our Capsule will patrol to and from. Now we must create our Capsule and make it patrol.

- In the Hierarchy View, right-click and select **3D Object>Capsule**.

- Reposition the **Capsule** so that it is just above the Terrain (its Y value should be approximately 1).

- With Capsule selected, right-click in PlayMaker View's Graph View and select **Add FSM**.

- With **FSM** active in the Control Bar, rename **FSM** as **capsulePatrolFSM**.

- Select State 1 and with State active in the Control Bar, rename State as **moveTowardsA**.

- In the Graph View, right-click State moveTowardsA and select **Add Transition>FINISHED**.

- In the Actions View, search **moveto** and double-click on result **Move Towards**.

- In the Hierarchy View, click and hold and drag and drop GameObject **pointA** into the **Target Object** field in the Move Towards Action in the State Inspector.

- Specify **Finish Event** as **FINISHED** (Figure 22.3).

- In Graph View, right-click State moveTowardsA and choose **Copy States**.

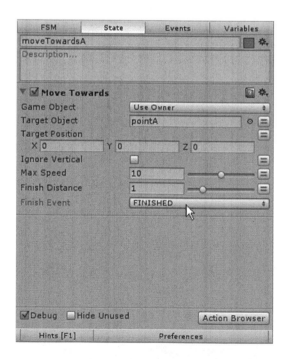

FIGURE 22.3   The correctly configured Move Towards Action.

- Right-click elsewhere in the Graph View and select **Paste States**.

- In the **Replace Start State** dialogue, select **No**.

- Rename the pasted State as **moveTowardsB**.

- In the Hierarchy View, click and hold and drag and drop GameObject **pointB** into the **Target Object** field in the Move Towards Action in the State Inspector.

- Specify **Finish Event** as **FINISHED**.

- In Graph View, click **FINISHED** and drag a Link into the opposite State and click the other **FINISHED** Transition and drag a Link into its opposite State (Figure 22.4).

It is always a good idea to hit Play and test things out every once in a while. Barring any mishaps, the Capsule should patrol as intended. Let's create our placeable turret. We will want it to follow the mouse pointer around. That will involve getting the mouse pointer's coordinates from "on" the terrain, saving them as a variable, and then placing the turret at the location specified in the variable. We will need to do this every frame so that the turret does indeed follow the mouse pointer. Let's begin.

- In Hierarchy View, right-click and select **3D Object>Cube**.

- Repeat, this time creating a **Sphere**.

- Repeat, creating another Sphere.

- Repeat, this time creating a **Cylinder**.

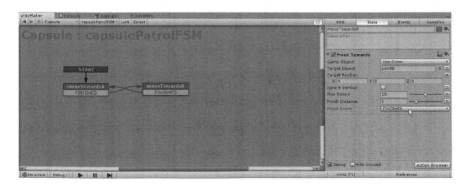

FIGURE 22.4   Correctly configured capsulePatrolFSM.

- Rename the Cube **turret**.

- Rename the first Sphere **missile**.

- Position the second Sphere so that it juts halfway out of the top of the turret.

- In the Inspector View, in the **Transform** Component, specify the Cylinder's **Scale** as 0.3, 0.7, 0.3.

- Specify the Cylinder's **Rotation** as **0, 90, 90**.

- Position the Cylinder so that it is shallowly embedded in the Sphere and points to the lower left-hand corner of the View.

- In the Inspector View, in the Transform Component, specify the missile's **Scale** as **0.3, 0.3, 0.3**.

- Position the missile at the visible end of the Cylinder (Figure 22.5).

- In the Hierarchy View, drag Sphere onto turret to child it.

- Drag missile onto turret to child it.

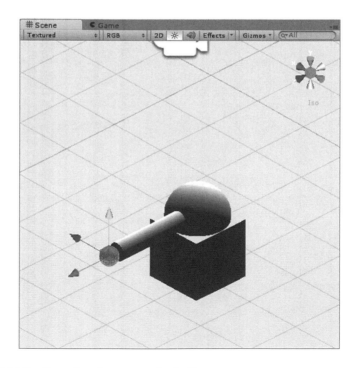

FIGURE 22.5 Completed turret and missile.

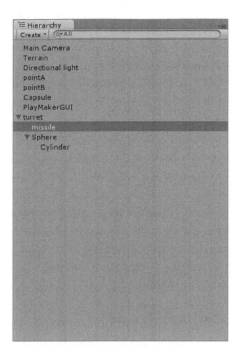

FIGURE 22.6   The correct parent/child relationships.

- Drag Cylinder onto Sphere to child it (Figure 22.6).

- With turret selected, right-click in Graph View and select **Add FSM**.

- Rename the FSM as **turretControlFSM**.

- Rename **State 1** as **movingTo**.

- With **Events** active in the Control Bar, **Add Event toPlacement**.

- Right-click State movingTo in the GraphView and **Add Transition** toPlacement.

- With **Variables** active in the Control Bar, add **New Variable** "**turretPlacing**," define its **Type** as **Vector3**.

- Check the box next to **Inspector**.

- In Actions View, search for and add Actions **Mouse Pick**, **Set Position**, and **Get Mouse Button Up** to the movingTo State.

- Note that the Actions must be listed in the same order in the State Inspector as they are in the book; execution order is super important.

- In **Mouse Pick**, specify **Store Point** as variable turretPlacing.

- Check **Every Frame**.

- In **Set Position**, specify **Vector** as variable turretPlacing.

- Check **Every Frame**.

- In **Get Mouse Button Up**, specify Send Event as **toPlacement**.

So far, so good! The turret should follow the mouse movement. Now we want to make its placement permanent. This is the same procedure as getting the mouse "coordinates" *once* and placing the turret at those coordinates *once*. Essentially, we'll be using the same Actions as before, we just won't update them Every Frame.

- In Graph View, copy State movingTo and paste it.

- Rename the newly pasted State as **placement**.

- In the placement State, uncheck **Every Frame** in both **Mouse Pick** and **Set Position**.

- Delete Action **Get Mouse Button Up**.

- In Graph View, right-click State placement's **toPlacement** Transition and select **Transition Event>FINISHED**.

- Note that none of the Actions in placement reference an (Transitional) Event; FINISHED is both Action and Transition, causing the procedure to automatically flow into the next State once all Actions have completed.

- Right-click in Graph View and add State **fire**.

- In Actions View, search for and add **Actions Activate GameObject** and **Look At**.

- In Activate GameObject, in the **GameObject*** row, select **Specify GameObject** and into the resulting field drop **missile**.

- In Look At, drag **Capsule** into the **Target Object** field.

- In Graph View, drag a Link from toPlacement to placement and from FINISHED to fire (Figure 22.7).

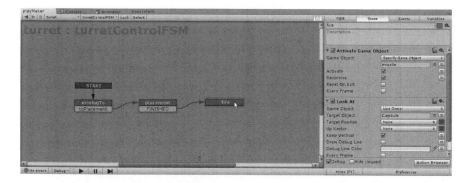

FIGURE 22.7   The completed FSM.

There is just one constituent missing an FSM now: the missile. Before we complete **missileGuidanceFSM**, let's give our Scene some color. Previously, it was stated that materials are a combination of textures and shader specifications. Briefly, it was mentioned that you can create a Material without a texture map in Unity. We will just do that now.

- In **Assets**, create a folder named **Materials**.

- In Materials, right-click and select **Create>Material**, then name it **red**.

- In the Inspector View, click the white swatch in the **Main Color** row.

- In the resulting **Color** window, select a red color.

- Repeat these steps creating a **blue** and a **yellow** Material.

- Drag Material blue onto the words **turret**, **Sphere**, and **Cylinder**.

- Drag Material red onto the word **Capsule**.

- Drag Material yellow onto the word **missile**.

Everything is a little brighter. Let's give our missile guidance.

- With missile selected, right-click in the Graph View and **Add FSM**.

- Name the FSM **missileGuidanceFSM**.

- Rename **State 1** as **moveTowards** and add the **Move Towards** Action.

- Create the Event **toDestruction**.

- In Move Towards, specify the **Target Object** as **Capsule**.

- Specify the **Finish Event** as **toDestruction**.

- In Graph View, create the State **destruction**.

- With State destruction selected, search for and add the **Activate GameObject** twice.

- In the first Activate GameObject Action, in the **GameObject*** row, select **Specify GameObject** and into the resulting field drop Capsule.

- Uncheck the **Activate** box.

- In the second Activate GameObject Action, in the **GameObject*** row, select **Specify GameObject**, and into the resulting field, drop missile.

- Uncheck the **Activate** box.

- Note that these Actions *must* deactivate their respective Game-Objects in the order mentioned above or it will not work; if missile deactivates first, it will never have a chance to deactivate Capsule.

- In the Inspector View, uncheck the box next to missile to begin the Scene with the missile deactivated (Figure 22.8).

- Hit Play.

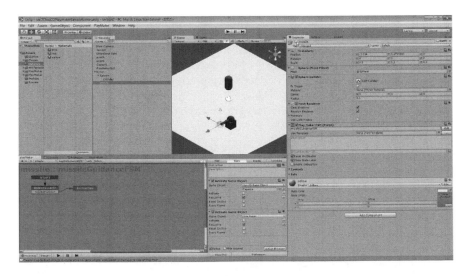

FIGURE 22.8   The scene thus far.

- Note that there is something really wrong.

- Exit Play Mode dejectedly.

22.1 TROUBLESHOOTING

There is a problem. The turret attacks *us*, not the Capsule. The turret is in the wrong place. Something is wrong with either how the turretPlacing variable gets its coordinates or how the turret is being assigned the turretPlacing variable coordinates. Let's first examine how turretPlacing gets its coordinates. It receives its coordinates from Mouse Pick; we will begin there.

If we click on the Help icon in the Mouse Pick Action Editor, it will take us to PlayMaker's online manual where we will receive information about Mouse Pick. The first few lines read as follows:

> Perform a mouse pick on the scene and store the results. Use Ray Distance to set how close the camera must be to pick the object. NOTE: This action uses the Main Camera.

What this is telling us is that Mouse Pick beams a ray from the mouse pointer into the scene and records what it hits (BTW, it is also telling us that if turretPlacing never updates with coordinates, it may be that Main Camera is too far from Terrain). We are using Store Point. Regarding Store Point, the manual says.

> Store the point of contact.

This means it stores the point coordinates of whatever it hits. In our scene, we are storing the point of whatever the ray hits in turretPlacing and moving our turret there. What is happening is becoming clear.

The first time the cursor is moved, it will most likely hover over Terrain. Mouse Pick's ray will hit Terrain, get the coordinates, and move the turret there. Now, however, the turret is blocking the terrain! Mouse Pick's ray will then hit the turret! The ray hits turret's outer mesh, gets the coordinates, and moves the turret's pivot point there. The result is that turret quickly lurches closer and closer to the Main Camera!

What we need is a way for Mouse Pick to ignore hitting the turret and only interact with Terrain. You may recall that we use Layers to add exceptionality. Let's do that now.

- In the Inspector View of any GameObject, select **Add Layer...** from the **Layer** rollout.

- In **User Layer 8**, type **terrainOnly**.

- In the Hierarchy View, select Terrain.

- In Terrain's Inspector View, select terrainOnly from the **Layer** rollout.

- Select **turret**.

- In the **movingTo** State, in the **Layer Mask** field of the **Mouse Pick** Action, type **1**.

- From the resulting rollout, select terrainOnly.

- In the **placement** State, in the Layer Mask field of the Mouse Pick Action, type **1**.

- From the resulting rollout, select terrainOnly.

- Hit Play.

It should work as intended. The turret follows our mouse movements and is placed when the user left-clicks. After being placed, the missile appears and seeks and destroys the capsule. It should go without saying that after playtesting, you should exit Play Mode and save the Scene.

What we have here is the beginning of a tower defense game. In addition to more and better meshes, textures, and special effects, it would benefit from UI, sound effects, and additional variables. Variables such as health, credits, points, and damage would serve to complete the tower defense game. Though incomplete, this Scene is a triumph of which you should be proud. With just six different Actions, we were able to engineer a relatively sophisticated game mechanic in an amazingly, blazingly short amount of time!

In our sample scene, we gained familiarity with several important game creation procedures. We learned that we need only a few common Actions to form a fully functioning game. When things went wrong, we were able to reason through to a solution. Thus, this concludes Section II. By now, you are probably salivating at the possibilities. In the next section, we will make those possibilities real as we begin to create an FPS survival horror game. See you there!

III

First-Person Shooter Survival
Horror Game Creation

CHAPTER 23

Indie by Design

A s mentioned earlier, game engines (e.g., Unity) and digital distribution have made independent game development economically viable. State machines (e.g., PlayMaker) make indie game creation possible for a whole new generation of developers. But what is indie? Is it simply a synonym for self-publishing? Or is a philosophy that entails seeing an artistic vision to completion, without the intrusion of crass commercial concerns? The latter definition begs the questions: Are games art? And, further, what is art?

These questions are far too big and much too boring to answer here. A better question is, what makes a game fun? What will make my indie game good and/or successful? Now, note that all of these considerations depend upon the game's completion. In turn, this means that the most important question of all is, how do we see this thing through to the end?

Let's start with a couple of definitions. By the end of my game development course at university, I was always sure to elicit the following definitions:

- **Game development is logistics. It is figuring out what needs to be done and doing it.**

- **Indie game development means getting it done within spirit-crushing time/money constraints.**

So, just how do you complete such a technically demanding product without money and hardly any time? A top-shelf game, circa 2005, costs

FIGURE 23.1   Good assets or bad assets, it's all the same in the dark.

approximately 120 man-years to create.* Today, a similar AAA title might cost more than a combined 400 years. How do you compete with that? The answer is start small and plan well. Good game design is the answer.

Let's deconstruct one of the most well-designed indies in all of gamedom's history, the survival horror game Slender: The Eight Pages (also developed in Unity). In Slender, you wander through the woods at night, playing from a first-person perspective. Your objective is to find Eight Pages without inadvertently finding Slender Man. Gaze upon him for too long and he will turn your screen to static! It is hard to describe in words why this is scary. Rather than ask what makes it scary or good, which are both subjective, we will look at what makes it *possible* (Figure 23.1). We will accomplish this by scrutinizing the developer's choices and determining the advantages thereby leveraged.

The Flashlight: The flashlight is a good example of starting small. Implementing a flashlight narrows the game world to a single point of light. Instead of attempting an expansive world of next-gen visuals and breathtaking vistas, the Slender dev rightly slashed his art asset needs to the bone. This is important because art assets are typically the most expensive aspect of game development. Here, the game's world is whittled away to not much more than what can occur in a

* Keith, C. *Agile Game Development with Scrum.* Upper Saddle River, NJ: Addison-Wesley, 2010.

two-feet radius at any given time. When the flashlight goes out, the art asset quantity and quality burdens are reduced to nearly nothing.

The Woods: Trees are like crates. Nobody gives them a second look, so nobody much cares how next gen or not they appear. They are just obstacles; players immediately head for the negative spaces in-between. Best of all, they are free and easy to implement in Unity. How easy? Button-pressed easy. We will see that trees can be procedurally generated in Unity.

The Gun: What gun? Yes, the conspicuous lack of a gun primarily serves as a negative mechanic, a technique of addition through subtraction. Its absence adds to the player's sense of claustrophobia, panic, and helplessness. It also functions as subtraction through subtraction, however, further reducing both the art asset and programming burden. No gun means no gun mesh and no gun textures (plural), and no firing animation. No hand mesh, no hand textures, no hand animation. No reload animation for either the hands or the gun. No ammo manager and no need to Raycast. No health manager for Slender Man. No hit animation. No death animation. No particle effects such as blood splatter. No need for a muzzle flash sprite. No need for additional dynamic lighting. That the game is less needy in terms of programming and art asset resources means it is likewise less needy in terms of system requirements. This allowed it to download quickly and run on low-spec PCs thereby making it highly accessible.

The Slender Man: The Slender Man appears as if instantiated from nowhere, always behind you, just out of sight. Creepy yes, but more importantly, efficient. Having the Slender Man appear out of thin air and just stand there means no path finding and eliminates the many challenges of implementing a rudimentary, yet fraught, AI. He does not have to move anywhere, figure out how to get around things, or really do much of anything. This means less programming, yes, but it also means doing away with animations.

If there has been a theme up to this point, it is that less is more. With proper planning, the developer smartly pared the game down to a most simple mechanic: "run" from a relentless movie monster (and then trimmed it even further by not having anyone actually *run* much). Good game design made Slender: The Eight Pages possible, first and foremost, and the fun followed.

But what made it successful? We touched upon its low-spec accessibility. This, in a small way, helped propagate its distribution. After all, the biggest problem an indie developer will encounter is not technical; it is promotional. Believe it or not, lots of anecdotal evidence as well as scientific study hold out that it is better to have good publicity than it is to have a good game.* Exposure will make or break a game, just ask Zachary Barth. Who? Exactly. Publicity is perhaps Slender's most brilliant coup. The character was an internet celebrity well before the game. Better yet he is folklore, devoid of any licensing fees. Every Slender Man search becomes potential publicity for the game of the same name.

Now, none of this is to imply that our earlier deconstruction serves as a checklist guaranteeing success. Sprouting trees all over the place and naming your game after something popular will only get you so far (in fact, SEO-naming tactics can have unintended consequences, even backfire†). It does go to show just how important good game design is, however. For the independent developer, that often means taking a small idea and making it smaller. Too often novice developers begin with a laundry list of art assets, equating "more" with "more better." Instead, begin with a mechanic that has an objective. For Slender, that would be "avoid terrifying monster." Note that the developer's objective of terrifying the player is different from the player's objective of gathering all eight pages. Wandering through the forest collecting pages is the player's means to the developer's ends. Once you have the mechanic and objective, you must resist its embellishment. Instead, work hard to figure out how to achieve the objective as simply and quickly as humanly possible. Then pare that idea further.

We now have some very practical definitions regarding indie game development. We deconstructed Slender Man: The Eight Pages and learned that less is more. Starting out small makes completion possible. We also learned that "small" is relative; today's "small" is inclusive of some fairly sophisticated games, including basic first-person shooters. In the next chapter, we will put that learning to good use as we analyze our project's game design document.

---

* Sliwinski, A. EEDAR/SMU study: Review scores affect perceived quality, purchase intent. Joystiq. com. N.p., July 6, 2010. Web. December 30, 2014.

† Seznec, Y. Gentlemen! or, how our most successful game is also our least profitable. Gamasutra. com. N.p., August 13, 2013. Web. December 30, 2014.

CHAPTER 24

Design Document

I N THIS CHAPTER, WE will look at the design document for our final project, the FPS Survival Horror Game *Get To The Choppa!* The document is accompanied by an in-line analysis in bold. The analysis consists of reasoning transplanted from the previous chapter as well as fresh insight.

I am sure you have heard it before; a design document is the blueprint you use to build your game. There is no standard format, but there are standards. Your design document must clearly convey to your future self, collaborators/employees, and potential investors exactly what to expect. No surprises. A good design document should allow for freedom as to *how* things are accomplished, but there should be no ambiguity about *what* needs to be accomplished.

Get To The Choppa!
Design Document

Table of Contents

Do not confuse this or any particular design document for a template. As mentioned previously, there is no standard format. The Table of Contents will vary from game to game. Even on a per game basis, the final design document may bear little resemblance to its former self. It should be amended and updated as development progresses. By the time I am ready to show the design document to potential investors, it will be complete with screenshots and marketing information. The brevity of this design document reflects the purposefully limited scope of the game as initially envisioned.

24.1 GAMEPLAY SYNOPSIS

Get To The Choppa! is an FPS Survival Horror video game. It involves running from and fending off a lethal cyborg ninja. The cyborg teleports in at random and attacks the player. The player can fend off the cyborg by shooting it, at which point the cyborg teleports out and waits to try again. The objective is to find and escape to a singular home-free location.

If this were part of a pitch, I might tell the investors, sometimes rightly renowned for their limited imagination, to think of this game as "The Predator Meets Slender Man."

24.2 NARRATIVE SYNOPSIS

In *Get To The Choppa!*, the player is investigating some sort of disturbance at his company's underground, secret AI research facility. He quickly realizes that their prototype robot has gone mad and killed everyone. When we join the story, the player is trying to escape by getting to an extraction point. In the core version, the narrative is explained through a HUD. In the expanded version, the player learns the plot through exposition (dialogue).

The core version is made up of the bare minimum number of elements we need for a playable Build. Although the term has come to mean different things to different people, this is also often referred to as a Minimal Viable Product. An indie developer should work toward that and naught else until its completion.

24.3 GAME MECHANICS

Get To The Choppa! is an FPS Survival Horror video game. It involves running from and fending off a lethal cyborg ninja. The cyborg teleports in at random and attacks the player with a katana. The player can fend off the cyborg by shooting it, at which point the cyborg teleports out and waits to try again. The win condition is fulfilled by making it across a dark tropical island to an extraction point.

In this example, the *Game Mechanics* introduction is little more than a reiteration of the *Gameplay Synopsis*. The *Gameplay Synopsis* is slightly less specific so that readers are free to imagine how the gameplay objectives might best be accomplished.

24.3.1 Gameplay Mechanics: Core Version
Player:

- The player is armed with a semi-auto handgun with a single extended clip.

Remember when I said to start small and make it smaller? This is that. "A single-extended clip" pays multiple dividends. It means no pickups (less code, less animations, less art assets) and no reloads (less code, less animations, less art assets, and, most [less] of all, less troubleshooting when it all goes wrong). Limited ammo also helps to define the game as survival horror and adds to the difficulty and, by extension, the dramatic tension. Limited ammo is actually more work for us than unlimited ammo; however, so this feature will not be implemented by the time we first begin playtesting.

- With a single successful shot, the player can fend off the cyborg (the cyborg will teleport away).
- The player must make it to the helipad to win.

Enemy

- The cyborg cannot be killed.
- The cyborg ninja teleports in at random intervals to one of three/four randomly chosen spawn points. Teleportation is/is not accompanied by a sound.

Here, I anticipate that teleportation might need to have an accompanying sound effect in order to give the player some warning that the cyborg is attacking. At this point, I haven't decided whether to have an

accompanying sound effect, but it is important to make a note of the consideration here.

- The cyborg jogs silently toward the player and attacks with a sword.

- A successful sword attack will kill in one/two/three hits.

Here, I am not sure how many hits should kill the player. One hit means less scripting but might be too frustrating for the player. Playtesting will sort this out.

- Getting hit by a bullet will cause the cyborg to teleport away.

Note that while I previously mentioned a seemingly minor detail such as a single sound effect, I am neglecting to mention other sound effects or art assets. In the instance of the particular sound effect mentioned above, it has a major gameplay consequence necessitating its inclusion here. Most other art assets are not so lucky. Having no unique gameplay consequence means they are not included in *Gameplay Mechanics*.

Environment

- The player is on a deserted tropical island at night. There is a mountain in the center.

This section will need to be revised when we decide to level the island and add a volcano.

- On the other side of the island is a helipad. When the player reaches the helipad, the player will win the game.

24.3.2 Gameplay Mechanics: Expanded Version

What would we do if we have the resources to make our game all that it can be? Now is the time to dream big. Dream big, but dream responsibly.

Player

- In addition to a handgun, the player has a walkie-talkie with which to communicate to the extraction team/helicopter pilot.

This means a whole lot more coding and art assets. Assuming we are developing this solo, we will have to find voice actors. That may mean shelling out money.

- Once the player makes it to the helicopter, the player can receive more powerful weapons with which to kill the cyborg.

Again, this means a whole lot more coding and art assets. Even if we wind up expanding our gameplay, we may have to omit this feature.

Enemy

- The cyborg teleports in silently but is semitransparent.

What a great way to increase the tension. Hopefully, there is a PlayMaker action that will allow us to manipulate transparencies.

- When hit once, the cyborg becomes completely visible but starts to run at the player.

What another great idea. Now this is a game I want to play.

- When hit a second time, the cyborg teleports away and waits to respawn.

Environment

- At the start of the game, the player emerges from an underground research facility.
- Instead of a fixed-location helipad, a helicopter spawns randomly at one of the three/four/five locations on the other side of the mountain.

This is great for the replayability of the game. Moreover, we should be able to reuse the PlayMaker Templates we create to randomly spawn the cyborg ninja to randomly spawn the extraction point.

- The player can communicate via walkie-talkie, asking the helicopter pilot to send up a single flare to denote the pilot's position.

While this may seem to defeat the mechanic of randomly spawning the extraction point, the volcano's eruptions will obscure the flare.

The player will deduce the necessity of getting to the other side of the volcano in order to capitalize on the flare mechanic.

- Extraction features a fully animated cutscene.

24.4 PLATFORM/CONTROLLER ASSIGNMENTS

Get To The Choppa! is to be built for PC and Linux. The controller assignments are standard FPS controls as played on a computer. WASD keys will move the player forward, back, left, and right. Strafing can be accomplished as well. The mouse will allow the player to look and aim all around. A left-click fires the gun.

24.5 GAME PROGRESSION

The first screen will be a title screen with a "start" button and text explaining the narrative/objective. The game will load and the game mechanics will play out. Either a game over or a win screen will be made to appear as a result of the game's conclusion. In the expanded version, start, game over, and win screens will feature animated cutscenes and voice acting.

24.6 MISCELLANEOUS

This is where I would keep notes. Speaking of notes, note that I avoided using pronouns in the design document. Pronouns can lead to confusion. Always be specific. Note too that your design document should have a footer. The footer should clearly mark your intent to reserve copyrights, the creation date, and revision number. This is to make sure that everyone is on the same page, both literally and figuratively. If I were sharing this document under a nondisclosure agreement, I would also make sure to mark every page as "Confidential Information." Avoid custom fonts for business documents, but if necessary, be sure to save the resulting document as a .pdf so that words do not go missing.

To recap, there is no standard format for design documents, but there are standards. This design document clearly conveys to my future self and anyone following along exactly what to expect. At the same time, it allows for creativity. *Get To The Choppa!* is a short game of limited scope and so its design document is likewise short.

CHAPTER 25

Our First Level (But Not Really)

I N THIS CHAPTER, WE will build our first level. We will tackle setting up the following: directional light, skybox, terrain, water, and foliage. We will import all the packages we will need for the entire section here in this chapter. Let's get to work.

- Create your "section3" Project.

- Download course materials from **http://nickelcitypixels.com/ noCodeBook/dlc.zip** and unzip the contents to a folder named **section3Assets** (this folder *must* be located *outside* of your section3 Project folder, and if possible, locate it on a partition other than the one in which your OS is installed).

Import the following standard projects into your **section3** Project:

- Character Controller

- Particles

- Scripts

- Skyboxes

- Terrain Assets

Import the following Custom Packages as well:

- Elementals

- PlayMaker

- PlayMaker Ecosystem (tinyurl.com/PlayMakerEco)

- PlayMaker Animator Proxy (obtained through PlayMaker Ecosystem)

- PlayMaker U Gui Proxy Full (obtained through PlayMaker Ecosystem)

- section3

- Terrain Toolkit (tinyurl.com/terrainToolkit)

- Water FX

- Water + Lite (this Package has recently transitioned from being free to paid; it is not absolutely necessary to implement this package)

Terrain begins its life as a plane but comes equipped with enough components and adjustable parameters to turn into rolling fields, canyons, crevasses, mountains, or all of the above and much more. Terrain is your game's ground. Because just about every game needs ground, Unity makes it quick and easy to implement.

- Create a new Scene, save it as **sec3Chap25OurFirstLevelPractice**.

- Select **GameObject>3D Object>Terrain**.

- In the **Terrain (Script)** Component, click the sprocket icon and then change **Resolution** to 1000 (**Terrain Width**) by 1000 (**Terrain Length**) (Figure 25.1).

- Rename Terrain to **Island** in both the Inspector View and Project View (single click **New Terrain** and wait patiently for it to become editable).

Unity measures distance in **Unity Units**. Unity Units can be whatever you would like, but it is typical to envision them as meters. Doing so means that our terrain is 1 km^2.

Unity's Terrain tools are a mixed bag. The Raise/Lower Terrain tools (represented by the icon of a mountain and an up arrow) in particular are of little use. The brush sizes are inadequate and there is literally very

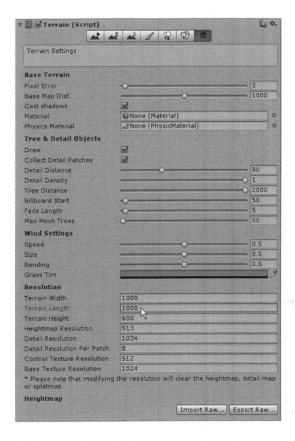

FIGURE 25.1 The Terrain (Script) Component being edited so that the Resolution is 1000 × 1000.

little middle ground. You can paint either high ground or low ground, but getting something in between, for example, a gentle slope, is difficult. For that reason it is best to use a **Heightmap** and/or use **Terrain Toolkit** to generate and edit terrain procedurally. **A Heightmap is a grayscale image that is used to store and represent height data where black represents low elevation and white represents high elevation**. Heightmaps are hand painted in an image-editing program or processed from real-world cartography images/data (Figure 25.2).

- In the **Terrain (Script)** Component, under **Heightmap**, click on **Import Raw...** and import "islandTerrain.raw" specifying 512 × 512 for **Width** and **Height**, **Windows** as the **Byte Order**, and 1000, 600, 1000 for the terrain size.

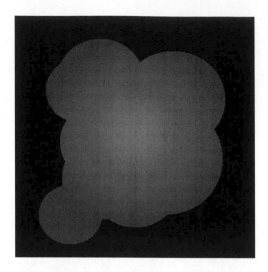

FIGURE 25.2   Heightmap islandTerrain.raw, created in Photoshop.

- Apply the **Terrain Toolkit** Component to **Island** either by dragging and dropping the **Terrain Toolkit** C# script from the **Terrain Toolkit** folder onto Island or by selecting Island in the Hierarchy View and clicking **Component>Terrain>Terrain Toolkit**.

- In the **Terrain Toolkit (Script)** Component, with **Create** and **Smooth** buttons depressed in the Control Bars, specify 3 as the **Iterations** parameter and click **Smooth Terrain** (Figure 25.3).

- Note that the terrain is smoothed over.

- With Create and **Fractal** buttons depressed, set the **Preset** parameter as **Rolling Plains** and the **Blend (strength) Parameter** as 0.3 and click **Generate Fractal Terrain**.

- Now your terrain has convincing characteristics.

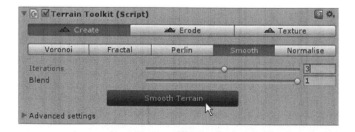

FIGURE 25.3   The Terrain Toolkit Component with its Smooth parameter edited.

A note on naming conventions: most of the time, if you see a button whose function is not entirely clear given the context (e.g., blend, opacity), it is safe to assume that it controls the strength of the associated effect.

One of the Terrain Toolkit's greatest features is the ability to procedurally texture Terrain according to the Terrain's slope. We are going to specify two textures, **grass** and **cliff**. With the press of a button, Terrain Toolkit will apply the textures, and where the terrain's slope is greatest the grass texture will give way to cliff texture. We will have realistic-looking terrain in less than 5 minutes.

- In the **Terrain Toolkit (Script)** Component, with the **Texture** button depressed in the topmost Control Bar, click **Add Texture**.

- Click where it says "Select" in the corner of the checkerboard image.

- The **Select Texture** window pops up in which you should select the first **Cliff (Layered Rock)**.

- Click Add texture.

- Repeat the process selecting the second **Grass (Hill)** texture for the second texture slot.

- Set the **Cliff start** parameter as 15 and the **Cliff end** parameter as 27 (Figure 25.4).

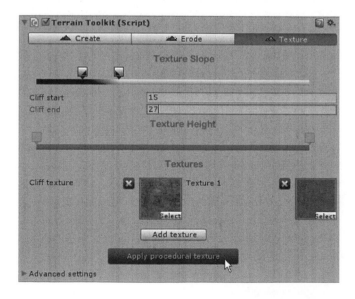

FIGURE 25.4   The Terrain Toolkit Component with its Texture parameters edited.

- Click **Apply procedural texture**.

- We have realistically textured terrain in less than 5 minutes.

Now where the terrain slope is the steepest, we have rock peeking through and elsewhere lush grass. We will transition back to Unity's Terrain tools now to implement its very useful **Place Trees** functionality. Much like Terrain Toolkit's procedural texturing, Place Trees will procedurally generate vegetation.

- In the **Terrain (Script)** component, select the icon of the two trees in the Control Bar.

- Click the **Edit Trees** button and in the **Add Tree** window, click the selection target icon.

- In the **Select GameObject** window, select the second **Palm** tree mesh (Figure 25.5).

- In the Add Trees window, click **Add**.

- Click **Mass Place Trees** and specify 20,000 trees in the resulting window.

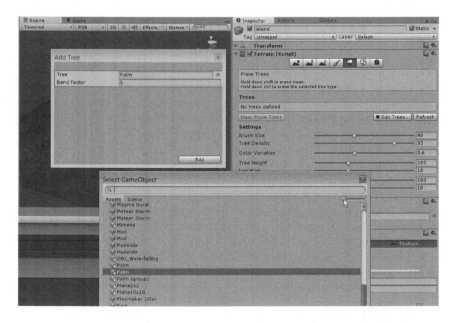

FIGURE 25.5   Here we see Unity with the Add Tree and Select GameObject windows open and with the previous parameters selected.

- Your trees have now been mass placed.

- Remove the trees from the ocean floor by setting the **Brush Size** to 70, holding Shift, and painting over the trees that are below what will soon be sea level (Figure 25.6).

- Click Edit Trees, then Add Tree, and select and add the **Fern** game object.

- With Fern selected in the **Trees** icon list, use the brush tool to paint in some Ferns.

- In **Assets>Terrain Assets>Bushes**, create the folder **Ambient-Occlusion**.

- Drag Fern into the new folder, right-click it, and select **Reimport**.

- Now your island is a tropical island.

We need a sky. There are several ways to apply a skybox, but there is only one way to ensure it will show up in the Scene View.

- Click **Edit>Render Settings**.

- In the Render Settings Inspector, click the Target Selection icon next to **Skybox Material**.

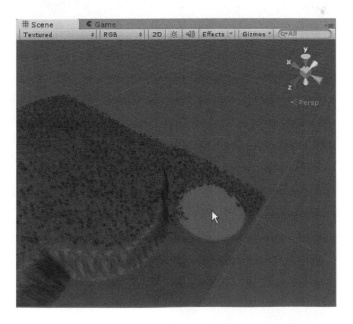

FIGURE 25.6   Illustrates the Scene View's current state and the act of tree erasure.

- In the **Select Material** window, select **MoonShine Skybox**.

- In the Scene View Control Bar, make sure **Effects** has been activated.

- Your game now has a sky!

Your island looks great! Or at least it would if it could be seen. We will need to add a light. In the chapter on GameObjects, it was mentioned that Directional Light is a good stand-in for the sun. It can also be a good moon stand-in if we turn down its brightness.

- Select **GameObject>Light>Directional Light**.

- Dial the **Intensity** parameter down to 0.25.

- In the Scene View, position it so that the Directional Light more or less aligns with the image of the moon in the skybox.

- The Light has been let!

Note that the only Transform value of the Directional Light that affects how the Scene is lit is the Rotational Transform. Position has no effect. You could position the light below the terrain and it would still light it. Regardless, you should get in the habit of placing it more or less where the light source appears on the skybox. In addition to appearing more realistic, it will allow for suitable flare effects should you choose to use them.

An island is not an island unless it is surrounded by water. Even though water is a fairly common need, it is not provided by Unity unless you buy the Pro version (or use version 5+). If expect an asset to be included with Unity but find that it isn't, be sure to check the Asset Store. You can often find what you need there for little to no cost as part of a Package. Most of the time, what you need from such a Package comes conveniently pre-fabricated in (you guessed it) the form of a Prefab. Always seek out the Package's Prefabs, usually in a subfolder named Prefab.

- In the Project View, expand the **WaterPlusShader** folder.

- **WaterSurface** exists as a Prefab in this folder, select it.

- Drag WaterSurface into the Scene View and position it appropriately.

- Your island is now an island!

Our survival horror game has terrain, tropical vegetation, moonlight, sky, and water. But it lacks the appropriate survival horror atmosphere. Let's return briefly to Render Settings and create a fog effect (recall that in Unity 5, the settings are located in the Lighting View).

- Position the **Main Camera** so that the **Camera Preview** window displays the **Island**'s surface and trees.
- Enable Game View.
- Return briefly to **Edit>Render Settings**.
- Click the checkbox next to **Fog** and experiment with the **Color** and **Density** parameters.
- A fog effect has been created.

Fog is great for setting a fearful, claustrophobic mood. It enhances the player's experience but does little for us as developers. Recalling our previous Scene View lesson, let's disable the fog effect there so that we can see what we are doing. Keep in mind the fog effect will still be visible to the player.

- In the Scene View, expand the **Effects** rollout menu.
- Uncheck **Fog**.

Fog, as a Render Setting, is a rendering effect, not a game object. It obscures visuals in direct proportion to their distance from the camera. It makes objects unseen and, although evident in its effect, is itself unseen. In real life, however, you can see the fog itself; you can see the vapors shifting and moving. Fortunately, such an effect is available to us in the Water FX Pack.

- In the Project View, expand the **Water FX Pack** folder and the **Prefabs** folder.
- Since **VolumeSteam** exists as a Prefab in this folder, select it.
- Drag the VolumeSteam Prefab into the Scene View and position it wherever (Figure 25.7).

I really like this Particle Effect. I like it a lot.

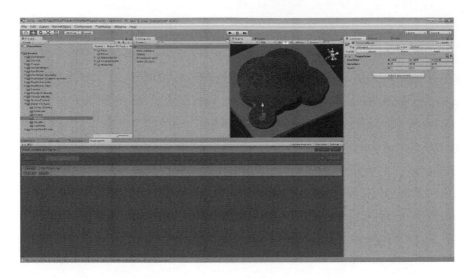

FIGURE 25.7   Unity's current state at the end of the chapter.

This chapter was momentous! We set up land, water, light, and sky. We textured our island with diffuse textures and populated it with foliage. We dabbled with fog as both a Render Setting and a Particle Effect. Best of all, it only took us a matter of minutes. In the next chapter, we will throw it all away. The good news is that, as always, I have prepared most of the Scene for you ahead of time.

CHAPTER 26

Level Redux

I N THE LAST CHAPTER, we created an island complete with water, sky, light, land, and vegetation. Then we added a Fog Rendering effect and a Fog Particle Effect. The latter effect was so successful as to suggest that it could define the level's overall aesthetic. Unfortunately, it is currently incompatible with our level. In this chapter, we will redo the level to accommodate the VolumeSteam Particle Effect.

The Fog Particle Effect, VolumeSteam, reflects the amorphous, shifting uncertainty of the horror-striken psyche. It is wraithlike, suggesting the presence of an otherworldly apparition. It should be perfect for our level but it is'nt, not yet. Particle Effects are relatively expensive in terms of the end user's system resources. Depending on whether or not the effect is culled when unseen, covering the island in VolumeSteam has the potential to cripple processing. What is the solution? We can create a sensibly sized VolumeSteam Particle Effect and have it follow the player. In that way, it will appear to be everywhere.

Unfortunately, the effect would still prove incompatible with our level. Recall that Particle Effects are simply textures on planes. VolumeSteam only gives the *illusion* of volume. If the player moves up or down through the Particle Effect, it will be revealed to be comprised of 2D planes and the illusion will be ruined. Even though we intend for the Particle Effect to move with the player, in practice, it will lag behind. The player will still move up or down through the Particle Effect as he/she traverses the slopes of our island. As mentioned earlier, this, will destroy the illusion. The solution is to level the level.

Unfortunately, leveling the level removes an integral obstacle. A game is not a game without obstacles. We will need to add an obstacle back in.

We will add an untraversable volcano. We have scheduled a lot of changes for our island; let's get to work implementing them.

- Open the previous Scene, **Save Scene as… sec3Chap26Level ReduxPractice**.

- Delete **Island** from the Hierarchy View.

- Add a New Terrain to the Hierarchy and set its Resolution to 1000 × 1000; rename it to **islandFlat**.

- Rename its Project View counterpart the same.

- In the **Terrain (Script)** Component, under **Heightmap,** click on **Import Raw…** and import **islandFlat.raw** specifying the same parameters as in the last chapter.

- Reposition (or consider deleting) **WaterSurface**.

- With islandFlat selected, attach the **Terrain Toolkit** component.

- Using **Terrain Toolkit (Script)**, smooth the Terrain specifying the same parameters as in the last chapter.

- Add another New Terrain to the Hierarchy and set its Resolution to 1000 × 1000; rename it to **islandFlatInverse**.

- Rename its Project View counterpart the same.

- In the Terrain (Script) Component, under Heightmap, click on Import Raw… and import **islandFlatInverse.raw** specifying the same parameters as was done previously.

- Uncheck IslandFlatInverse's Terrain (Script) Component.

IslandFlatInverse.raw was created by inverting the grayscale values of the **islandFlat.raw** image. By occupying **islandFlat's** negative space, **IslandFlatInverse** will prevent the player from falling off the edge of the cliff. Deselecting the **Terrain (Script)** prevents the mesh from rendering and being seen. Of course, its **Terrain Collider** script remains active.

- In Project View in **Assets,** create two folders; name one **Meshes** and one **Textures**.

- Import the **volcano.obj** into the Meshes folder.

- In the Scene View, position volcano in the center of the island (be sure to view it from multiple angles and ensure that it does not float in midair).

- Import the textures **volcanoNormals.jpg** and **volcanoDiff.jpg** into the Textures folder.

- In the Hierarchy View, expand volcano to reveal its mesh.

- Select the mesh; in its Material Component, specify the **Shader** as **Bumped Specular**.

- Click and hold and then drag and drop volcanoNormals into the **Normalmap** slot.

- An error message results; click **Fix Now** (Figure 26.1).

- Click and hold and then drag and drop volcanoDiff into the **Base (RGB) Gloss** (A) slot.

- Edit volcano's **Scale Transform** values so that they are 1.5 across the board.

- You now have a (inactive) volcano (Figure 26.2).

We are now ready to implement the Particle Effect as currently envisioned. Part of that vision involves childing VolumeSteam to the player's character model. We are not ready to implement the player's character model yet however. Instead, we will use "programmer art" to stand in for the character model.

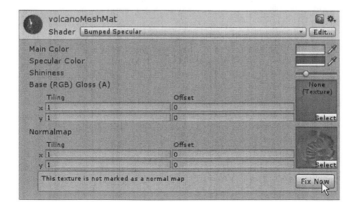

FIGURE 26.1 Volcano_normals occupying the Normalmap slot and the resultant error message.

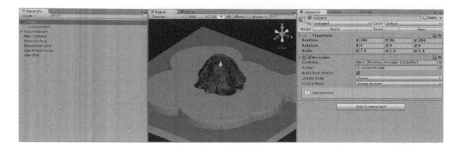

FIGURE 26.2   The volcano thus far.

Unfortunately, we will encounter a problem if all we do is child VolumeSteam to our character model stand-in. As our player moves forward, VolumeSteam will move with it, which is good. As our player turns however, VolumeSteam will turn too, which looks weird. So, we are going to use a PlayMaker FSM that causes VolumeSteam to follow the player around.

- Create an empty GameObject and name it **fpsCharFolder**.

- Position fpsCharFolder so that it is slightly above the surface of the island and midway between the island edge and the volcano.

- Create a **Capsule** GameObject and name it **fpsCharStandIn**.

- Child fpsCharStandIn to fpsCharFolder and edit its Position Transform values so that they are 0 across the board.

- Create an empty GameObject and name it **volumeSteamTarget**.

- Child volumeSteamTarget to fpsCharStandIn and in Scene View, position it at the center of the base of fpsCharStandIn's capsule mesh (Figure 26.3).

FIGURE 26.3   The locations of volumeSteamTarget in Hierarchy and Scene Views.

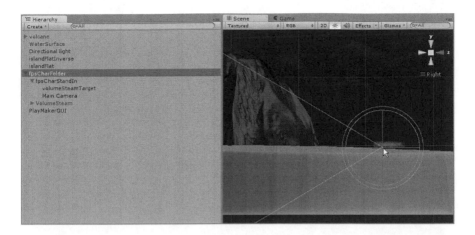

FIGURE 26.4   Parent/child relationships in Hierarchy and Scene Views.

- Now, child **VolumeSteam** to fpsCharFolder (not fpsCharStandIn and not volumeSteamTarget) and edit its Position Transform values so that they are 0 across the board.

- Child **Main Camera** to fpsCharStandIn and position it at the top of the Capsule (Figure 26.4).

- Ensure fpsCharStandIn and Main Camera's **Rotation** are both 0, 0, 0.

- Rotate fpsCharFolder so that it faces the volcano.

- Select VolumeSteam and in PlayMaker View, **right-click to add FSM**.

- In the PlayMaker View Control Bar, activate **FSM** and name it **followGameObject**.

- Select **State 1** and rename it **moveTowards**.

- Add the Action **Move Towards**; specify the **Target Object** parameter as volumeSteamTarget, **Max Speed** as 50, and **Finish Distance** as 0 (Figure 26.5).

- Finally, right-click in the PlayMaker canvas and select **Save Template**.

- Name the saved file **followGameObjectTemplate**.

- Texture the new IslandFlat Terrain with diffuse maps and vegetation meshes as described in the last chapter.

- We now have a viable Fog Particle Effect, an island, and then some (Figure 26.6)!

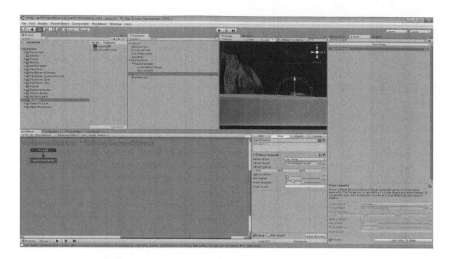

FIGURE 26.5   VolumeSteam's PlayMaker FSM.

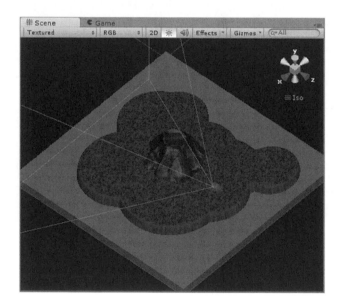

FIGURE 26.6   The Island thus far.

In this chapter, we redid our island to accommodate our VolumeSteam Fog Particle Effect. That involved creating a **followGameObject** FSM, leveling the island, and importing and texturing a volcano mesh. However, our accommodations do not end there; including a volcano promises lava. In the next chapter, we will deliver on that promise by learning how to make Particle Effects from scratch.

CHAPTER 27

Particle Effects

I N THE LAST CHAPTER, we created a whole new island to accommodate
our VolumeSteam Fog Particle Effect. We scripted it to follow the character model stand-in and leveled the island. This in turn meant adding a
landscape obstacle back into our map in the form of a volcano. In turn, that
necessitates the creation of a Lava Particle Effect. The easiest way to include
a Particle Effect is, of course, to use premade Prefabs that someone else has
created for us (like VolumeSteam). In this instance however, we must create
our own Particle Effect from scratch. We will do just that in this chapter.

Particles, to reiterate, are a series of planes that use partially transparent materials. They appear; they can move, rotate, change color, and scale,
and then they disappear. Let's create a Particle System now.

- Open the previous Scene, **Save Scene As... sec3Chap27Particle
EffectsPractice**.

- Select GameObject>Particle System.

- Position the Particle System just above the volcano mesh in Scene View.

- Create another Particle System and position it similarly.

- Name one system **lavaEmbers** and one system **lavaSpout**.

- Select lavaEmbers and inspect the **Particle System** Component
(Figure 27.1).

In the Inspector View, you can see that there are multiple **Sub-Components**
within the **Particle System** component, each with parameter piled upon

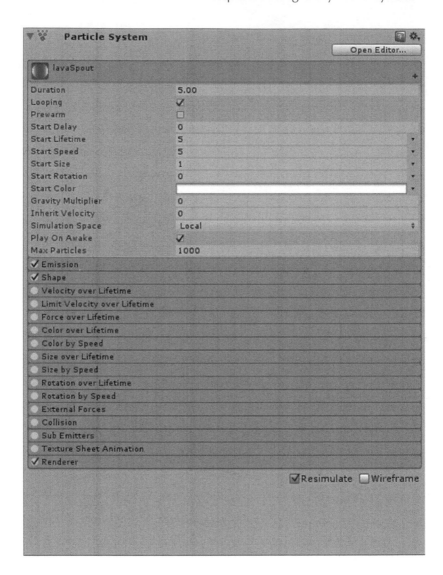

FIGURE 27.1 The parameters involved in defining a Particle System.

parameter. Some Sub-Component options elicit additional windows with even more parameters. Particle Systems can be overwhelming which is probably why many people opt to buy them as Prefabs straight from the Asset Store. Like most things however, Particle Systems become less intimidating the more you know about them.

In Particle System, **Shape**, and **Emission** Sub-Components, you should be aware of the following settings:

Duration defines how long a single cycle of particle emission lasts. Rate directs how many particles are emitted during Duration. Start Lifetime defines how long an individual particle lasts until it disappears. Max Particles defines the total amount of particles that can be on screen at any given time. The parameters in the Shape Sub-Component set the width and shape of the overall Particle System. Start Speed not only alters the speed at which individual particles travel but also serves to modify the height of the Particle System. You can probably foresee that Particle Systems suffer from the "too-many-dials problem." Particle System settings work in concert and one will often override the other. For example, if Max Particles is set to 5, it will limit the amount of particles on screen to 5, no matter if your Rate is set to 10. Settings may have unexpected results; for example, Start Speed has the potential to alter not only particle speed but the overall volume of the Particle System. In the end, Particle Systems are more art than science and you will have to experiment with settings until you get a desired look and "feel." To get the look and feel of lava embers, begin with the following:

- Select **lavaEmbers**.
- Set **Duration** to 11.
- Ensure **Looping** is checked.
- **Start Lifetime** should be 2.
- **Start Size** should be 10.
- In **Emission**, set **Rate** to 100.
- Max Particles should be set to 500 just to be safe.
- In the Shape Sub-Component, ensure **Shape** is set to **Cone**.
- Set **Angle** to 15.
- Set **Radius** to 70.
- Ensure that the particles **Emit from: Base**.
- Specify **Start Speed** as 200.
- Note that the height of the Particle System cone increases as well (Figure 27.2).

We want the particles to resemble embers. They will need to both shrink and fade away. This is accomplished in the **Color over Lifetime** and **Size**

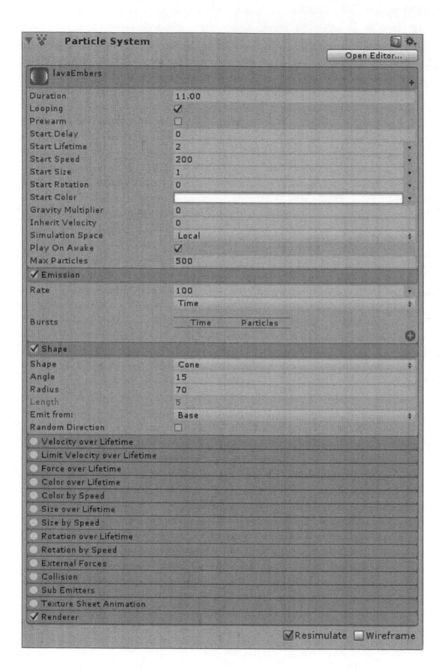

FIGURE 27.2 Pictured here is the Particle System Sub-Components: Particle System, Emission, and Shape with the appropriate settings for lavaEmbers.

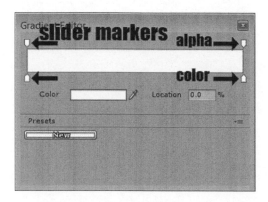

FIGURE 27.3   The Gradient Editor Window with the slider markers labeled.

over Lifetime Sub-Components. Make sure that they, and all the Sub-Components referenced in this chapter, are checked active.

Expanding the Color over Lifetime Sub-Component elicits a gradient editor launcher. Clicking on it launches a **Gradient Editor** Window (Figure 27.3). Initially, it displays a linear gradient map and irregular pentagons serving as slider markers. There is also a **Color** picker and a **Location** field in which to describe a slider marker's location as a percentage of the gradient map.

The slider markers along the top of the gradient map determine alpha (opacity) and the slider markers along the bottom determine color. You can add slider markers by clicking either near the top or bottom of the gradient map, and the markers can be slid by dragging them left or right. They are deleted using the delete key.

- Open the **Gradient Editor** Window as described earlier.

- Select the leftmost alpha slider marker and set its Alpha value to 0.

- Repeat with the rightmost alpha slider marker.

- Add an alpha slider marker at the midpoint of the gradient map by clicking at the midpoint of the top of the gradient map.

- Set its Alpha value to 180 (Figure 27.4).

Expanding the Size over Lifetime Sub-Component elicits a graph editor thumbnail. Clicking it does nothing (without having the Particle System Curves editor expanded). However, clicking **Open Editor...** at the top of

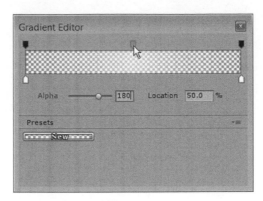

FIGURE 27.4   The Gradient Editor Window configured with the proper parameters.

the Particle System Component launches a **Particle Effect View** in which all Sub-Components can be selected. If you now click the graph editor thumbnail in the Size over Lifetime Sub-Component, it elicits a graph editor in the right-hand panel of the Particle Effect View (Figure 27.5). At the bottom of the graph are presets.

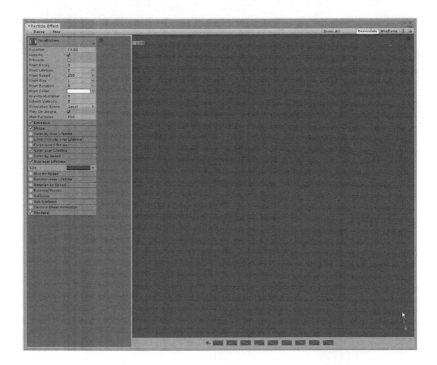

FIGURE 27.5   Particle Effect View with the Size over Lifetime Sub-Component selected and its graph edited with the mouse pointer engaging the bezier curve handle.

- Select the third preset from the right.

- Increase the fall off rate by selecting the end point and manipulating its bezier curve handle.

We can imbue our Particle Effect with additional visual interest by making it rotate as well as shrink and fade. This is accomplished in the Rotation over Lifetime Sub-Component.

- Enable and expand the **Rotation over Lifetime** Sub-Component.

- Assign **Angular Velocity** the value of 45.

We will now change the texture of the particle. Instinctively, you will most likely want to click on the texture thumbnail to change it. After all, it is clearly labeled **Select**. This portion of Unity's interface is misleading, perhaps even poorly designed. It is good to identify user interface failings like this so that you, as a developer, become conscious of what not to do. Do not label something "Select" and then not have it be selectable. We will have to access alternate textures in an alternate manner.

- Expand the **Renderer** Sub-Component.

- Click the target selection icon next to **Material**.

- In the Select Material window, select **Smoke**.

Unfortunately, our new Particle System is incompatible with our Scene. It may appear to be operating correctly in the Scene View, but that is only when Lighting and Fog Rendering Effects are both deactivated. In-game, Fog will obscure our Particle System. Previously, the existence of Self-Bright textures (aka Unlit Textures) was mentioned. These are textures that (should) glow in the dark. Troubleshooting would reveal that most Unlit Materials, while unaffected by lighting conditions, are not unaffected by Fog. They are likewise obscured. Researching the manual and online forums suggests that we will need to create a custom shader for our particles to shine through the Fog. Because this is a no-code course, I have created the Shader for you. Its creation, however, was trivial enough that anyone can do it. It involved taking an existing Shader, searching for the word **Fog**, replacing **Color (0, 0, 0, 0)** with **Mode Off,** and then renaming the script. As another option, you could search through all the Shaders for existing **Fog {Mode Off}** code, but for you, there is an even easier alternative to both these methods.

- Import **unaffectedByFog.shader** into the Standard Assets>Shaders> Particles folder.

- Assign **unaffectedByFog.shader** as the Material's Shader by clicking and holding and then dragging and dropping the script onto the Shader selection drop-down (alternately by selecting it from the Shader selection drop-down by navigating to Custom>unaffectedByFog).

- Assign an orange **Tint Color**.

- You now have a convincing lavaEmbers Particle System.

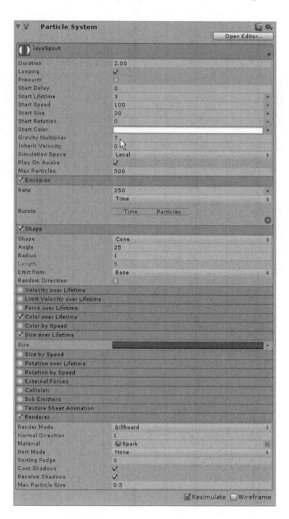

FIGURE 27.6   LavaSpout's Particle Effect View with the Velocity over Lifetime Sub-Component selected and its graph edited.

Knowing what you now know about Particle Systems, you should be able to create lavaSpout on your own. It is very much like lavaEmbers except that it has slightly different Particle System attributes including a tint that is more reddish. **Gravity Multiplier** is responsible for the lava emissions' arc. Loop staggering can be created through differential Duration and Start Lifetime parameters.

- Select the **lavaSpout** Particle Effect.

- Match its parameters with those shown in Figure 27.6.

- You now have an active volcano!

In this chapter, we created Particle Effects from scratch. While the amount of Particle System parameters seems mind-boggling at first, learning of their underlying effects quickly made them manageable. In the next chapter, we will finalize our volcanic activity by adding a light source.

CHAPTER 28

Lighting

I N THIS CHAPTER, WE will complete our volcano by creating the illusion that its red hot lava is casting light. Perhaps more than any other aspect of Unity, lighting suffers from the "too-many-dials" problem, which will be addressed. First, however, we will need to learn some technology and some terminology.

The movie industry has the luxury of prerendering its CGI animations. Hollywood studios use warehouses of high-end computers to draw frames of animations days at a time. The game industry has no such luxury. A video game must calculate and render graphics right before the end users' eyes. Instead of rendering frames days at a time, video games typically render 60 frames every single second. To ensure that calculations perform quickly, developers simplify things by using the simplest shapes possible: triangles. All the meshes in a 3D game are made up of triangles. As the end user's processing power increases, so does the number of triangles that can be manipulated in real time. Even today, however, that upper limit of triangles *still* is not enough to give the illusion of photorealism. Thankfully, some very intelligent people came up with a work-around: Normal Mapping.

Normal Mapping is based on the premise that calculating the physics for a mesh's triangular geometry is very expensive but certain aspects of lighting it is not. What Normal Mapping does is first ascertain lighting information from a high-poly mesh. That information is projected onto a lower-poly (less triangles) mesh that is used in-game. The game then lights the low-poly mesh using data generated from the prerendering. This trick lighting gives the low-poly mesh the illusion of having greater geometry than it actually has! The magical set of data used for the trick lighting is saved as a texture image of the type, you may have guessed it: Normal Map. Note that as with all things related to textures, Normal Maps go by multiple names. They are also known as **Bump(ed) Maps**.

Normal Mapping is a fascinating, revolutionary technology and the reason modern games are able to have photorealistic graphics. If you are not a game artist however, you do not have to worry too much about it all. To ensure a mesh looks realistic, a Unity game developer needs to know/ do three things:

1. Make sure your game always includes the proper Shaders.

2. Specify each mesh's Normal Map in the Normalmap slot of the Material editor (and "Fix Now" if necessary).

3. Make sure that Unity's settings and lights play nice.

Here is where our "too-many-dials" problems begin. Let's enumerate some of the dials.

Recall that textures are only one part of the material equation. In addition to what to render, we need to specify how things should render; we do that with shaders. That is possible if, and only if, Unity decides to put the shader instructions that we need into the game's final build. We will need to ensure that Normal Map Shader decisions are not left up to Unity or the end user.

- Open the previous Scene, **Save Scene as... sec3Chap28 LightingPractice**.

- Expand **Always Included Shaders**.

- Select **Edit>Project Settings>Graphics**.

- In the Inspector View, denote **Size** as one more than is currently specified.

- Click the selection target icon next to the newest **Element** and in the **Select Shader** window choose **Bumped Specular** (Figure 28.1).

That is dial number one. Dial number two involves making sure Unity's settings behave. There are two important lighting technologies: **Vertex**

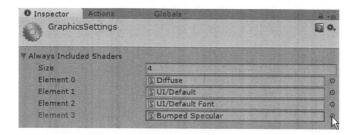

FIGURE 28.1   The Graphics Inspector View with the Select Shader Window open.

Based and "**Per Pixel.**" **Vertex Based means that Normal Maps *will not* work (but is less expensive in terms of system resources) and Per Pixel means that Normal Maps *will* work.** If you want realism, Normal Maps are necessary expenses. We will need to make sure that all of our settings and lights use Per Pixel.

- Go to **Edit>Project Settings>Player Settings**.

- In the Inspector, expand **Other Settings**.

Confusingly enough, the parameters Unity chooses to indicate Vertex Based or Per Pixel lighting attributes are not always labeled as such. Here in **Rendering Path**, the choices are **Vertex Lit**, **Forward**, and **Deferred Lighting. Vertex Lit is recognizable. Selecting it means that Normal Maps will not work. Deferred Lighting ensures that Normal Map lighting will always be enforced, but it only works with Unity Pro. Forward means that we get to choose how the lights behave on an individual basis. We need to enable this to get Per Pixel lighting to work.**

- Expand the **Rendering Path** rollout.

- Select **Forward** if it is not already selected (Figure 28.2).

Dial number three is actually a number of dials equal to the number of lights you have. Their render type can be set individually. Before we fiddle with dials, let's create our Volcano's light.

- Select **GameObject>Light>Spotlight** and position it above the volcano.

- Set its **Range** to 200.

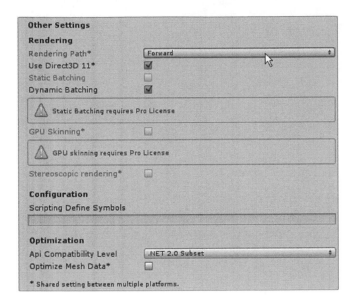

FIGURE 28.2   The Player Setting's Inspector View with Forward Rendering Path selected.

- Set **Spot Angle** to 70.

- Choose an orange hue for its **Color**.

- Set its **Intensity** to 8.

Confusingly enough, the parameters Unity chooses to denote Vertex Based or Per Pixel lighting attributes are not always labeled as such. Deja vu. In a light's Inspector View, the setting is **Render Mode** and the choices are **Auto, Important**, and **Not Important. Important means that Normal Maps will always work. Not Important means that Normal Maps will never work. Auto means that Unity will prioritize either graphics fidelity or performance; sometimes Normal Maps will work, sometimes they will not.**

- Select the **Spotlight**.

- Set **Render Mode** to **Important** (Figure 28.3).

Dial number three is not as important as its parameters suggest. The next dial can override it. It sets a cap on how many Important (Normal Maps work) Lights there can be in a scene.

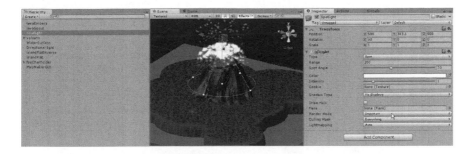

FIGURE 28.3   Point light selected with its Render Mode set to Important.

- Select **Edit>Project Settings>Quality**.

- Ensure **Good, Beautiful**, and **Fantastic Levels** have their **Pixel Light Count** specified as 4 (Figure 28.4).

Levels are performance/graphics quality presets that the end user can select when they run the game. It may not be a bad idea to pare the presets down to something more easily manageable. Presets can be deleted by clicking the trash can icon.

Those are the most common dials that must be properly set to enable Per Pixel (Normal Maps work) lighting. Keep in mind that there may be others. For example, if you introduce a package that has extremely high performance requirements, it may introduce new dials into the mix or simply override Unity's. Augmented and virtual reality–related packages are good examples of those that may set hard limits on Per Pixel rendering.

Let's revisit the options available to our Point light. The effects of many settings such as **Range, Color, Intensity** (strength), and **Shadow Type** should be obvious. Others are slightly less so.

Cookie uses a texture map and projects the map's image as if it were a patterned gel covering the light.

When checked, **Draw Halo** creates a semitransparent glowing "sphere" around the light source. Candles and fireflies are good examples of light sources made more convincing by halos.

Flare mimics a lens flare effect, that is, visible light artifacts meant to convey that the source light is blindingly bright.

Culling Mask allows you to select whether GameObjects of a certain Layer should or should not receive light. By default, **Everything** is selected and as a result, everything will receive light.

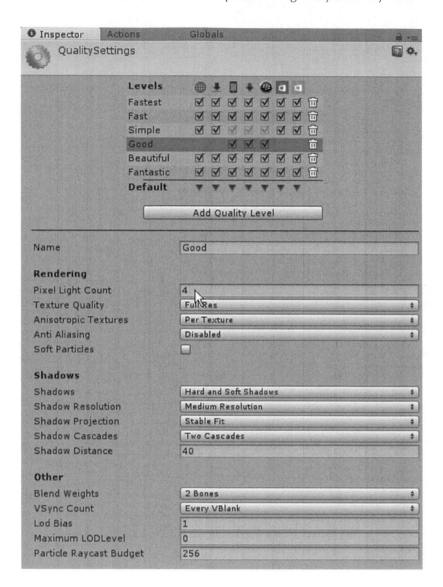

FIGURE 28.4 The Quality's Inspector View with Fastest selected and Pixel Light Count set to 4.

Lightmapping allows you to choose **RealtimeOnly** or **Baked**. Baked Lightmapping necessitates Unity prerender the Scene's lighting, save the information to a texture image file, and then overlay the texture data onto the GameObjects in the Scene. The advantage is that lighting calculations are done ahead of time. This improves performance. The downside is that the lighting is static (and for our purposes, is too time-consuming). Baking Lightmaps is an excellent way to optimize most games' performance. It is not necessary for a game with a minimal number of lights however. Our project is one such game.

28.1 TROUBLESHOOTING

It might seem safe to assume that by now, our lighting is working as intended. It is not.

- Rotate characterFolder until the top of the volcano is visible in the **Camera Preview** picture-in-picture when Main Camera is selected (a Camera gizmo denoting **Field of View** will help you to aim).

- Note that the top of the volcano is not lit in Camera Preview.

- If Scene View's Fog Effect is unchecked, check it.

- Note that the top of the volcano is lit in Scene View but not in Camera Preview (Figure 28.5).

In Scene View, even with the Fog Rendering Effect active, the top of the volcano appears lit. This suggests that the culprit is not the Fog Rendering

FIGURE 28.5   Here we see discrepancies in lighting between the Scene View and Camera Preview's picture-in-picture.

Effect. Perhaps, the in-game lack of lighting has something to do with Culling Masks.

- Expand **volcanoLo** and select its mesh, **volcano**.
- Note volcano's **Layer Mask**.
- Select **Point light** and note its **Culling Mask**.

Since volcano uses a default Layer and Point light's Culling Mask is set to Everything, it should be receiving light.

- Move the Point light near the characterFolder.
- Note that Camera Preview shows palm trees being lit.
- Move the Point light back over the volcano.

Either we have been misled by the fact that the volcano appears lit in Scene View (even with the Fog Rendering Effect active) or we have been misled by culling masks and the volcano mesh is some sort of lighting exception.

- Select Edit>Render Settings.
- Uncheck **Fog**.
- Note that the volcano now appears lit in Camera Preview.

It seems that Scene View misled us and the Fog Rendering Effect was the culprit once again. We need to find a middle ground between a Fog Rendering Effect and being able to see the lighting effect.

- Set **Fog Mode** to **Linear**.
- Note that the volcano now appears lit in Camera Preview and we are achieving a nominal Fog Rendering Effect.
- The volcano looks (not sounds) complete.

Unity 5 has taken steps to mitigate the too-many-dials problem as it relates to lighting. Other aspects of lighting have been improved as well.

In this chapter, we learned all about lighting and put that information to good use. Audio, by comparison, will be simple.

CHAPTER 29

Audio

I N THIS CHAPTER, WE will complete our volcano with audio and add
some other sounds. As with any additions, accommodations will be
needed to be made.

For better or worse, audio in game development is treated as something
of an afterthought. Many developers take it for granted that free audio art
assets will be available to them whenever they need. This sense of entitle-
ment is not wholly without reason; free music and sound effects are plenti-
ful. Moreover, the implementation of sound in Unity is trivial. Audio can,
in most instances, be completed as part of the wrap-up process. That is not
to say it should be however. We will get some sound taken care of ahead
of schedule.

Give a developer an art asset and he makes games for a day. Show him
how to make art assets and he will not *have time* to make games. It is best
to show him where the free art assets are. I get 99% of my audio from the
following sites:

http://www.soundbible.com

http://www.freesound.org

http://www.assetstore.unity3d.com

In addition to a plethora of free quality sounds, the sites do a great job
of documenting licensing rights. Internet media is not an everything-up-
for-grabs free-for-all. You must have permission to use any assets that are

not your own. Do the right thing. Remember, as a game developer, piracy threatens your livelihood!

- Open the previous Scene, **Save Scene as... sec3Chap29Audio Practice**.

- At soundbible.com or freesound.org, search for and download the following sound effects that have the appropriate copyright permissions; a single gunshot and a low rumbling (for the volcano).

- After realizing that there are no decent nighttime tropical island sound effects, search for and download the following sound effect that has the appropriate copyright permissions: rain or thunderstorm.

- Create a folder in Assets and name it **Sounds**.

- Import the downloaded sound effects as well as those included in **dlc.zip**.

In order to get sounds to function, a Scene needs two things:

1. A single **Audio Listener** Component

2. An **Audio Source** Component

Think of the Audio Listener as being a microphone attached to the Main Camera. That is the most common placement of the Component and is attached by default. **An Audio Source is just that**, **the source of a sound**. Sounds that follow the player around or otherwise play at a steady volume should be attached to the same GameObject that contains the Audio Listener (Main Camera). Otherwise, they should be attached to the GameObject responsible for the sound's "creation." If the sound should occur as the result of a particular condition (e.g., a gun firing), it can be played by a PlayMaker FSM; the GameObject will still necessitate an Audio Source Component however. There are many useful PlayMaker Audio Actions.

- Add two **Audio Source** Components to **Main Camera** (Figure 29.1).

- Click and hold and then drag and drop your rain or thunderstorm sound effect from sounds to the first Audio Source's **Audio Clip** field.

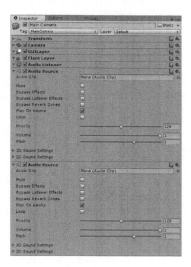

FIGURE 29.1   Main Camera's components.

- Click and hold and then drag and drop your low rumble sound effect from sounds to the first Audio Source's Audio Clip field.

- Edit both Components so that **Play on Awake** and **Loop** are checked.

It can be assumed that since it is a small island, the player would be able to hear the volcano from anywhere. Therefore, we have attached it to the Main Camera for playtesting purposes. It is one of the shortcuts that allows us to quickly arrive at a minimally viable game. If there is time, it will make more sense to attach the Audio Source to the volcano and edit its parameters so that it becomes louder with increasing proximity. This would be accomplished through **Volume** and **3D Sound Settings**.

Level design choices will sometimes be limited by the availability of art assets. Such is the case with our rain sound effect. A usable night-time tropical island sound effect is not available and having no ambient sound makes the Scene quiet, too quiet. Instead, we will be using rain to drive away the otherwise expected island animals and their accompanying noises. The addition of rain sounds however necessitates the addition of rain visuals. That means adding more particle effects, which will be addressed in a later chapter. For now, this chapter will content itself with introducing audio and having finally completed the volcano. In later chapters, we will play sounds on command using PlayMaker Actions.

In this chapter, we learned the basics of Unity audio engineering: download free sound effect, drag and drop it into an Audio Source Component, and edit its Volume and 3D Sound Settings or don't. With the addition of sound, we have completed the volcano and in doing so finalized VolumeSteam's necessary accommodations. In the next chapter, we will examine the extent of the cascading systemic disruption that VolumeSteam had on our level. We will also study how Mission Creep of this sort undermines our number one game development commandment: start small and work smaller.

CHAPTER 30

Moral to the Story

I N THE FIRST CHAPTER of this section, we succeeded in creating an entire island. Since then, we have just been recreating the island to accommodate the VolumeSteam Particle Effect. Hopefully, you can see how adding a single, seemingly simple feature can cause things to spiral out of control.

When we first decided to include VolumeSteam, it was difficult to foresee the ripple effect it would have on our level's design. First, we had to scrap the work we had already done in creating the island; work that had involved making Heightmaps, editing the Terrain with Terrain Toolkit, and texturing the island with diffuse maps and vegetation meshes. Then, new Heightmaps that leveled the island had to be created. We had to reedit and retexture the island. Leveling the island eliminated an important game mechanic: the obstacle of mountainous terrain. We added an obstacle back into the scene in the form of a volcano. Although this process may not have been evident, it meant sculpting a volcano (which in turn required artistic study and trial and error), painting it, creating a low poly, unwrapping it to create UVW coordinates, and rendering out normal maps and diffuse textures. A video game volcano is not a video game volcano without lava and so we had to create lavaEmbers and lavaSpout Particle Effects from scratch. There was a problem; the lava Particle Effects did not show up in game. This required troubleshooting to determine that the Effects were being obscured by the fog. The solution required a modicum of research and then a little coding. The volcano's lighting effect was likewise obscured by fog, which required additional troubleshooting and problem solving. Speaking of troubleshooting, there was also the troubling realization that simply childing VolumeSteam to the player's character model would cause it to turn when the player turned. Thankfully, this had a quick and easy solution in the creation of followGameObjectFSM, but it still cost time. Everything costs time and even little costs (and not so little costs) quickly add up. In the real world, the total process would easily add at least four days to the development budget. Four days would cost the studio head approximately $1250 per employee. Maybe it would add a week if the trial-and-error artistry and troubleshooting did not go smoothly. All of this work just got us back to where we were at the beginning of our development, all just to add a simple (premade mind you!) Particle Effect. There is a lesson to be learned here; start small and work smaller. A long list of frivolous features will put an end to forward progress. This in turn effectively ends development.

Whether VolumeSteam is a frivolous feature is up for debate. The good is that it defines the look and feel of the game. The bad is that it costs time, a lot of time.

Novice developers underestimate and underreport the costs involved in making a video game. Sometimes, this is part of an ill-conceived strategy.* As a result, the public is likewise ill-informed of the high costs of indie game development.† A further consequence is that early "successfully" crowdfunded indie games failed to deliver on their promises about 67% of the time.‡ These situations push price expectations lower and crowdfunding suspicions higher in a vicious cycle that is derailing indie game development viability.

The moral of Section III thus far is to be honest about your costs, especially with yourself. Anticipate and calculate costs carefully; then, double that sum. You can refine your cost expectations with experience. I recommend that you use a timer and extensively log the hours that you work on game development, noting particularly time-consuming aspects. After all, the self-deceived are the least likely to succeed and the last to know when they have failed. Keep on top of your time and money expenditures.

---

* Burgun, K. Kickstarter for the Average Indie. *Gamasutra Article*. UBM Tech, September 12, 2012. Web. September 02, 2015.
† Katie, C. "Big Indie" Kickstarters are killing actual indies. *Polygon. Vox Media*, May 19, 2015. Web. September 02, 2015.
‡ Subject, Un. Gamasutra: Un Subject's blog—A look at kickstarted video game delivery rates. *Gamasutra Article*. UBM Tech, February 25, 2014. Web. September 02, 2015.

CHAPTER 31

First-Person Shooter Controls

I N THIS CHAPTER, WE are going to begin the arduous process of getting our character to move and turn and strafe and look about. We will map his movements to the keyboard keys most commonly used by first-person shooters. We will also make sure that our character obeys the Scene's physics by adding colliders and collision detection. There is a lot to do; let's get started!

- Open the previous Scene, **Save Scene as... sec3Chap31FPS ControlsPractice**.

- Select **fpsCharStandIn**.

- In the **Inspector,** click **Add Component>Character>FPSInput Controller**.

- Note that several Components are added.

- In the Inspector, click **Add Component>Camera-Control>Mouse Look**.

- Hit **Play** in the Game View Control Bar.

- Play (Figure 31.1).

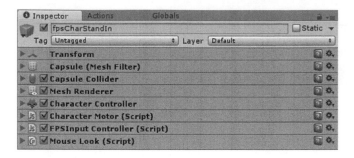

FIGURE 31.1   fpsCharStandIn with the FPSInput Controller and Mouse Look Components added.

31.1 TROUBLESHOOTING

Everything should be working correctly. If the fpsCharStandIn falls through the island into infinity however, be sure to check the following:

1. fpsCharStandIn should have the same World Space location by virtue of it being the child of fpsCharFolder and having 0, 0, 0 Position coordinates.

2. fpsCharFolder should be above the **islandFlat** Terrain.

Well, that was a freebie. In this chapter, we completed the arduous process of getting our character to move and turn and strafe and look about. In the next chapter, Random Spawn Manager *will* actually be quite involved.

CHAPTER 32

Random Spawn Manager

O UR CORE GAME MECHANICS involve a cyborg Ninja teleporting (spawning) near us and attacking. We can deter his attacks by shooting him, at which point he will teleport to safety only to try to attack us again. In this chapter, we will tackle this core mechanic by creating an FSM that will spawn the cyborgNinja randomly at one of three locations. We will also learn how to facilitate interconnectedness by using Global Transitions to receive messages from another FSM.

In order to create tension, the player cannot know from when or where the cyborgNinja will attack. This means we will have to randomize him both in terms of time and space. It is actually easier than it sounds. **We just need to break down this complex task into small, simple parts in a process known as stepwise refinement**. First, we need some programmer art. Let's create a stand-in for our cyborg Ninja. We will create a sphere and texture it as a self-lit soap bubble. We will deactivate our evil soap bubble; it is not ready to make its grand appearance yet.

- Open the previous Scene, **Save Scene as... sec3Chap32Random SpawnManagerPractice**.

- **GameObject>Create>3D Object>Sphere**.

- Rename the Sphere **cyborgNinjaStandIn** and position it under the map.

- In the **Inspector View**, with **Mesh Renderer** expanded, expand **Materials**, click the target selection icon, and select **SoapBubble**.

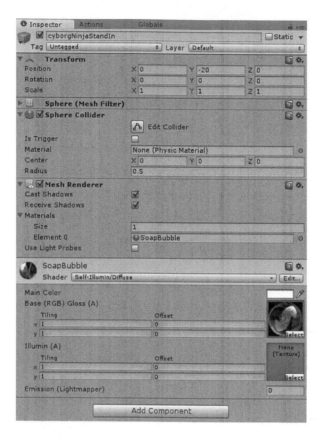

FIGURE 32.1   A correctly edited cyborgNinjaStandIn.

- In the Material editor, specify the **Shader** as either **Self-Illumin>Diffuse** or **Unlit>Texture** (Figure 32.1).

- Deactivate cyborgNinjaStandIn by clicking the first checkbox (the checkbox next to its name) in the Inspector View.

Now, we are going to create an empty GameObject, child it to fpsCharStandIn, and zero its Transform values. We are going to name it **spawnPointMarker** and give it a new Tag; **spawn**. The Tag is given so that we can randomly select from a number of empty GameObjects with the spawn Tag. With one spawnPointMarker selected among several, the FSM will know where to position our evil soap bubble. Obviously, this necessitates having multiple spawnPointMarkers. We will duplicate the spawn point (it has so few parameters that it is not worth bothering to make it a Prefab) and move each so that there are spawnPointMarkers in front of and to either side of fpsCharStandIn.

- **GameObject>Create Empty**.

- Rename the **Empty GameObject** as **spawnPointMarker**.

- Select spawnPointMarker and in the Inspector View, access the **Tag** rollout and select **Add Tag…**.

- In the **Inspector View**, specify the **Size** as 2 and type **Spawn** into the **Element 0** field.

- Select spawnPointMarker and set its Tag as Spawn.

- Child spawnPointMarker to **fpsCharStandIn** and specify its **Transform Position** and **Rotation** as 0, 0, 0.

- Duplicate (Ctrl+D) spawnPointMarker twice, naming the first duplicate **spawnPointMarker1** and the second duplicate **spawnPointMarker2**.

- Clear the area around **fpsCharStandIn** of foliage.

- From a top-down perspective, rearrange the spawnPointMarkers so that they are in front of and to either side of fpsCharStandIn (Figure 32.2).

Let's first envision a completed FSM and then go about creating it. In this first State, we are going to create a random number that is going to be the time at which our enemy should spawn. In the next state, we will check to see if our current time matches the random number we have chosen. If it does, great! We will go onto the next state where we spawn our enemy. If the cyborgNinja has been shot, we will need a Global Transitional Event enabling the FSM to rerun. Because the FSM will need to be active even when cyborgNinja is not, we will have to attach it to an Empty GameObject rather than the cyborgNinja itself.

- **GameObject>Create Empty** (outside fpsCharFolder).

- Rename as **randomSpawnManager**.

- Right-click to **Add FSM randomSpawner**.

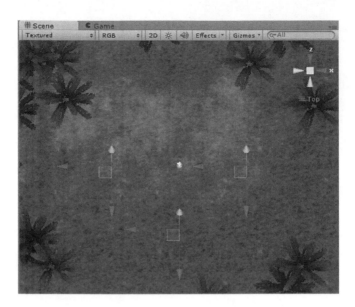

FIGURE 32.2 Pictured here is a composite image of spawnPointMarker GameObjects arranged around fpsCharStandIn.

- Rename the first State **clockBaslining**.
- In the Graph View, right-click to **Add State**.
- Name it **checkIfTargetTimeReached**.
- Right-click to Add State.
- Name it **randomSpawning**.
- Right-click to Add State.
- Name it **gameWin**.

Let's envision a completed first State before we go about creating it. We have identified that we need a random number that is going to be the time at which our enemy should spawn. We don't want it to be too random however; otherwise, we might choose −134.56 or 1,000,003. In the first instance, it would never be time for our enemy to spawn; in the second, our player would die of boredom before anything ever happened. What we need is a number that represents a time in the near future. That is, our slightly random spawn time should be equal to the current time plus some random number within a reasonable range. This can be accomplished with a float variable, the **Get Time Info** Action, and some float-related Actions. Let's create a variable.

- Click **Variables** in PlayMaker's Control Bar.

- In the **New Variable** field, type **timeSinceStart** and specify **Variable Type** as **Float**.

- Click **Add**.

- Checkmark **Inspector**.

- In the New Variable field, type **randomTimeTarget** and specify Variable Type as Float (you may need to click elsewhere to exit editing timeSinceStart).

- Click Add and checkmark Inspector.

- Select State **clockBaslining**.

- Add the Action **Get Time Info**.

- Set **Get Info** to **Time Since Startup**.

- **Store Value** should be timeSinceStart.

- Add the Action **Random Float**.

- **Min** is 5; **Max** is 10.

- Store **Result** in **randomTimeTarget**.

- Add the Action **Float Add**.

- **Float Variable** is randomTimeTarget.

- **Add** is timeSinceStart.

- Right-click the clockBaselining State and **Add Transition FINISHED** (Figure 32.3).

The Action **Float Add** may be somewhat confusing. Unless you are familiar with programming conventions, Float Add does not adequately explain what it is doing. At first glance, it seems as if it is simply adding two floats and neglecting to save the result into a variable. In actuality, the result is

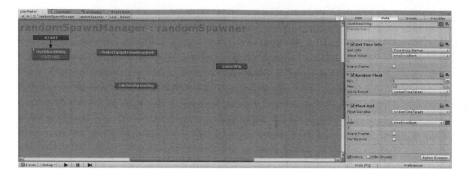

FIGURE 32.3 The correctly specified clockBaselining State.

being saved into randomTimeTarget. A variable is not its numerical value. A variable is just a container for a numerical value. **TimeSinceStart's value is added to randomTimeTarget's value, and then randomTimeTarget's is assigned the sum**.

In the next state, we will want to check when we reach our randomTimeTarget value. We will need to Get Time Info again to see what time it is. First, we should create an Event.

- Activate **Events** in the Control Bar.

- **Add Event toRandomSpawning**.

- Right-click and copy **Get Time Info**.

- Paste **Get Time Info** into checkIfTartgetTimeReached.

- Ensure **Get Info** is **Time Since Startup**.

- **Store Value** is **timeSinceStart**.

- **Every Frame** is checked.

- Add Action **Float Compare**.

- **Float 1** is **randomTimeTarget**.

- **Float 2** is **timeSinceStart**.

- Tolerance is 1.

- Specify **Equal** as toRandomSpawning.

- Every Frame is checked.

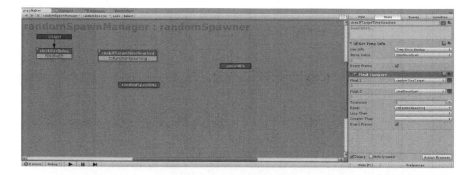

FIGURE 32.4   The correctly specified checkIfTargetTimeReached State.

- Right-click the clockBaselinedState and **Add Transition toRandomSpawning** (Figure 32.4).

We have one last State in the spawning process: **randomSpawning**. It will Activate our villain and move it to one of the spawnPointMarkers.

- Click **Variables** in PlayMaker's Control Bar.
- In the **New Variable** field, type **choosenSpawnPointMarker** and specify **Variable Type** as **GameObject**.
- Click **Add** and checkmark **Inspector**.
- With State randomSpawning selected, add Action **Activate GameObject**.
- **GameObject** should be set to **Specify GameObject**, and **cyborgNinjaStandIn** should be dragged and dropped from the Hierarchy View into the resulting field.
- Ensure that **Activate** is checked.
- Add Action **Get Random Object**.
- **With Tag** should be specified as **spawn**.
- **Store Result** should be specified as **choosenSpawnPointMarker**.
- Add Action **Move Towards**.
- **GameObject** should be set to **Specify GameObject** and specified in the resulting field as **cyborgNinjaStandIn**.

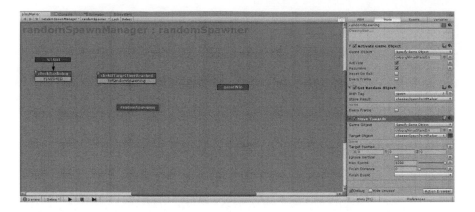

FIGURE 32.5   A correctly configured randomSpawning State.

- **Target Object** should be choosenSpawnPointMarker.
- **Max Speed** should be set to an inelegant 1000.
- **Finish Distance** should be 0 (Figure 32.5).

All that is left is to wire our States together. It should be straightforward and self-evident.

- Drag a Link from **Finished** to **checkIfTargetTimeReached**.
- Drag a Link from **toRandomSpawning** to **randomSpawning**.

Our randomSpawnManager should work correctly. Yet we still need to script accommodations for the player hitting the cyborgNinja and for the Player reaching the helipad and winning.

Games can be complicated. There is much interconnectedness. In PlayMaker, interconnectedness is facilitated by an FSM's ability to trigger another FSM's Event. To send messages to another PlayMaker FSM, use Send Event. To receive messages, it is best to establish Global Transitional Events.

- Activate **Events** in the Control Bar.
- **Add Event restart**.
- Check the checkbox next to restart to make it a Global Transitional Event (Figure 32.6).

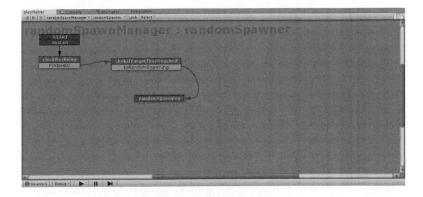

FIGURE 32.6   An illustration of the completed FSM.

- Hit **Play**.

- Observe from a top-down perspective in Scene View.

- After a few seconds, the evil soap bubble appears.

In this chapter, we took the complicated process of randomly teleporting the cyborgNinja about and broke it down into manageable tasks using a process known as stepwise refinement. We learned that to send messages to another FSM, we use the Action Send Event and that to receive messages, it is best to establish Global Transitional Events. In the next chapter, Mecanim will be discussed.

CHAPTER 33

Mecanim Preparation

Mecanim workflow is as such:

1. Imports the Model/Models (complete with animation files).

2. Translates the Model's external 3D modeling program's skeletal system to Unity's thus defining its Avatar.

3. Places the Model in the Scene View.

4. Creates and specify an Animator Controller (state machine) Asset.

5. Creates state machine States, Transitions, and Parameters similar to those in PlayMaker.

Mecanim is an expansive, complicated system (alternately described as "rich and sophisticated" in the manual). Like all other complicated systems in Unity, it often suffers from having "too-many-dials." The good news is that like PlayMaker, Mecanim is a state machine, and so while the interface is dissimilar, the underlying philosophy is the same. It does have some very valuable uses and it is worth the time and effort needed to learn it. In this chapter, we will cover steps one through four.

There are two ways to get animations into Unity: One is for the animator to create a single file that is composed of multiple animations. This file is then imported into Unity and the developer names and distinguishes the animations according to the key frames they occupy. The other way is for the animator to create a single file for each animation. Each animation is then imported into Unity individually. The files should abide by the following naming convention: meshName@animationName.fbx. The @ symbol lets Unity know that it is an animation file. In the section3 Project, the animation files will be imported individually.

- Open the previous Scene, **Save Scene as... sec3Chap33Mecanim PreparationPractice**.

- Create a **Models** folder in **Assets**, and then create a subfolder **cyborgNinja**.

- Into the subfolder, import the files **cyborgNinjaMaskAndEyes.fbx**, **cyborgNinja@Run.fbx**, **cyborgNinja@Hit.fbx**, and **cyborgNinja@ Attack.fbx**.

- Expand and examine cyborgNinja@Run.fbx (Figure 33.1).

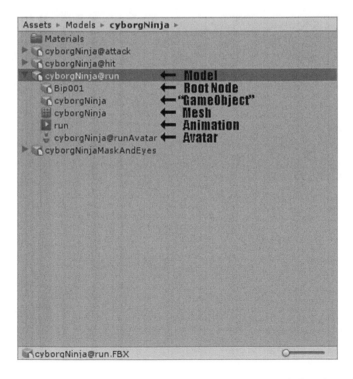

FIGURE 33.1 Here we see the file cyborgNinja@run expanded and its elements labeled.

FIGURE 33.2   Shown here is a character mesh rigged with a skeleton inside an external 3D modeling program.

The first cyborgNinja@Run, the one containing all others, is often referred to as the **Model**. Conceptually, it is a poorly constructed contraption. It cannot be properly referred to as a GameObject yet because it lacks Transform values; it is an Asset and a Prefab. It morphs into a GameObject once it is instantiated in the Scene. **Bip001** is the **Root Node** (pivot point or central bone) of the skeletal system as defined in its external 3D modeling program. The second (cube icon) cyborgNinja is the dormant cyborgNinja GameObject. The third (grid icon) cyborgNinja represents the cyborgNinja Mesh. **Run** is the animation (Figure 33.2).

In order to leverage efficiencies, humanoid characters use a skeletal system to drive their animations. This allows animators to reuse animations and programmers to create dynamic and physics-driven animations. Standard issue skeletons are much more easily manipulated than the unique meshes they inhabit. Standard issue is not so standard however; across software packages, there is some discrepancy as to which bone is named what. **The second step in Mecanim's workflow (after import) is to translate the 3D modeling software package's skeleton to Unity's skeleton system. This translation is saved in a file and is known as an Avatar. An Avatar can be used across multiple animations. Translations (Avatars) are done in Rig.**

- Select **cyborgNinja@run**.

- In the Inspector View, click to activate **Rig** in the Control Bar.

- In **Animation Type**, select **Humanoid**.

- Click **Apply**.

- Click **Animations** in the Control Bar (Figure 33.3).

- Note that in the Animations preview, contrary to Rig's animation preview, there is something terribly wrong with cyborgNinja's neck.

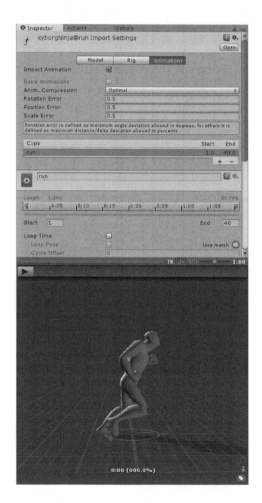

FIGURE 33.3   CyborgNinja has a crick in its neck.

33.1 TROUBLESHOOTING

This should be easy to troubleshoot. The cyborgNinja looks good in Rig, as it did in the external 3D modeling package. It looks bad in Animations, using Unity's skeletal system. Obviously, something has gone wrong in-between, in the translation process. While the automated translation process did a great job, it must have failed with the word "neck." We will need to manually correct the translation.

- First, save the **Scene** (it will prompt you in a moment and you will want to have already specified the correct name).

- Click **Rig**.

- Click **Configure** (Figure 33.4).

- To the left of the Humanoid image, select **Head**.

- Note that in the Neck field, the bone is unspecified (i.e., specified as **None [Transform]**).

- Click the target selection icon in the **Neck** field and specify **Bip001 Neck**.

- Click **Apply** and **Done**.

- Examine the results by clicking **Animations** in the **Control Bar**.

- You are a cyborgNinja chiropractor!

The cyborgNinja's Unity skeletal system has been corrected. Corrections can also be made by selecting the newly defined Avatar in Assets and then clicking **Configure Avatar** in the Inspector View. Let's add the cyborgNinja to the Scene.

- Select **cyborgNinja@Run** in the **Assets>Models>cyborgNinja** folder.

- Click **Model** and under **Materials**, uncheck **Import Materials** (in this instance, the imported file does not contain textures; they will be imported separately).

- Click **Apply**.

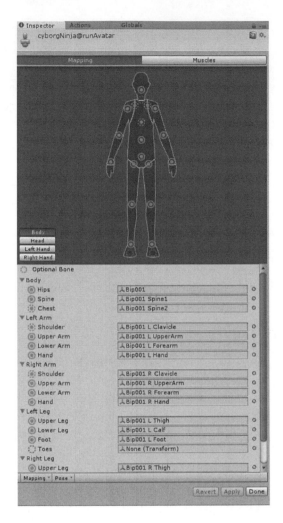

FIGURE 33.4   The Avatar Configuration editor in the Inspector View.

- Import the following textures into the **textures** folder: **cyborg-NinjaDiff.jpg**, **cyborgNinjaEyeDiff.jpg**, **cyborgNinjaMaskDiff.jpg**, **cyborgNinjaMaskNormals.jpg**, and **cyborgNinjaNormals.jpg**.

- Drag and drop the cyborgNinja@run Model into the scene and specify its coordinates as 0, 0.1, 0.

- Expand cyborgNinja@Run.

- Click and hold and then drag and drop **cyborgNinjaDiff** onto **cyborgNinja** in the Hierarchy View to enable the Material editor.

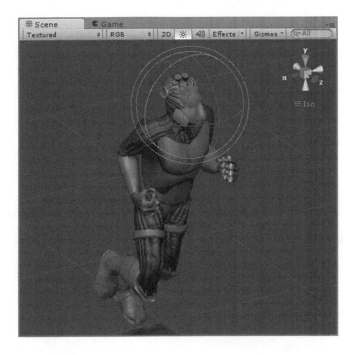

FIGURE 33.5 The hierarchy and proper positioning of cyborgNinja
MaskAndEyes.

- Select cyborgNinja and if necessary, click **Shader** in the Inspector View to expand the Material editor.

- Specify its **Shader** as **Bumped Specular**.

- Select **cyborgNinjaNormals** for the **Normalmap** slot; click **Fix Now**.

- Add **cyborgNinjaMaskAndEyes** to the Scene.

- Expand **Bip001** and subsequent Bip001 objects until **Bip001 Head** is exposed (it resides in the **Bip001 Spine1** tree).

- Child cyborgNinjaMaskAndEyes to Bip001 Head and then in Scene View, position it appropriately (Figure 33.5).

- Expand cyborgNinjaMaskAndEyes and select **cyborgNinjaEyes**.

- Assign cyborgNinjaEyes the **cyborgNinjaEyeDiff** texture.

- Specify **Self-Illumin/Diff** as the Shader.

- Select **cyborgNinjaMask**.

- Assign cyborgNinjaMask the **cyborgNinjaMaskDiff** texture.

- Specify its Shader as **Bumped Diffuse**.

- Select cyborgNinjaMaskNormals for the Normalmap slot; click "Fix Now."

The cyborgNinja is on the Scene and looks great! At least it would if we could see it. We will need to add a light.

- Create a **Point light** and position it in front of the **cyborgNinja** Model.

- Child it to the cyborgNinja Model.

- Set **Range** as 2; **Intensity** should be 1.

- Set the **Color** to red.

- Select the cyborgNinja Model and in the Inspector, create the new **Layer** "**cyborgNinja.**"

- Specify the cyborgNinja@run **Layer** cyborgNinja.

- Select **Yes, change children**.

- Select the Point light and specify its **Culling Mask** as only cyborgNinja.

- It is now looking good (Figure 33.6).

In anticipation of it needing to receive bullets, we will have to attach a Collider Component. This will enable collision detection calculations.

- Add a **Capsule Collider** to the cyborgNinja@run Model.

- In Capsule Collider, edit the **Center Y**, **Radius**, and **Height Parameters** so that the Collider completely envelops the **Model** (Figure 33.7).

Note that we didn't add a **Rigidbody** Component. While this would give our cyborgNinja convincing "physical" properties, it often introduces issues that the novice developer is ill-equipped to deal with. Issues such as bouncing (sometimes solvable by editing the Layer Collision Matrix), toppling over like a toddler (usually rectified by checking the **X** and **Z** boxes in

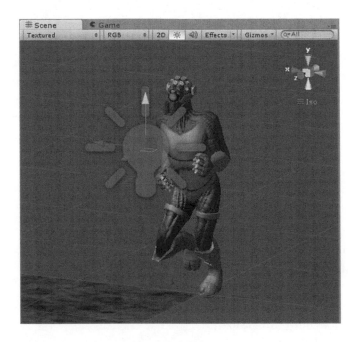

FIGURE 33.6   CyborgNinja textured and lit.

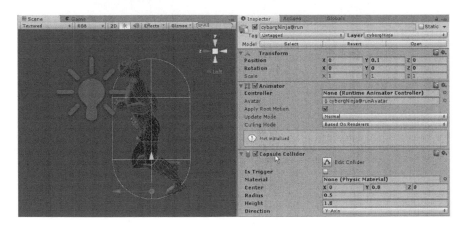

FIGURE 33.7   Here we see the cyborgNinja@run Model enveloped by the Capsule Collider and its Components exposed in the Inspector.

the **Constraints>Freeze Rotation** section of the Rigidbody Component), and inexplicably shooting off into space (try unchecking **Apply Root Motion** in the Animator Component) to name a few. Keep in mind that without a Rigidbody Component, our cyborgNinja is simply floating at a constant height like a lethargic helium balloon. The height at which it floats is dictated by its pivot point, which is currently roughly in the center of the bottom of its feet. We may need to employ a pivot point hack later.

The fourth step in the Mecanim process is to establish a state machine. For that, cyborgNinja@Run will need an Animator. By default, it comes with an Animator Component but lacks an Animator Controller, which is the state machine's Graph View. Theoretically, Animator Controllers can be used across Models. Each animated GameObject needs its own Animator Controller. Unlike just about everything else thus far, the Animator Controller is not found in the GameObject or Component menus. The Animator Controller creation button is located under Assets.

- While in the **Models>cyborgNinja** folder, select **Assets>Create> Animator Controller**.

- Name the **Animator Controller "cyborgNinja AnimatorController."**

- With **cyborgNinja@Run** selected, click the selection target icon in the **Controller** field of the **Animator** Component, and with the **Assets** tab active, specify cyborgNinja AnimatorController.

Now with our Components, Avatars, and Controllers all in place, we have all the magic keys necessary to unlock a functioning **Animator View**. Immediately, it will look familiar.

- Make sure to select **cyborgNinja AnimatorController** in the **Assets>Models>cyborgNinja** folder.

- Click **Window>Animator**.

- Dock the **Animator View** as a togglable tab next to the **Hierarchy View** (i.e., either Hierarchy or Animator View will be visible according to the tab selected).

- Consider saving this new arrangement as part of your **Custom Layout** (Figure 33.8).

In this chapter, we imported our Model, translated skeletal systems thereby creating an Avatar, placed the Model in Scene (and textured it),

FIGURE 33.8   The Animator View with Any State front and center.

and established an Animator Controller allowing us access to a working Animator View. In addition to Mecanim preparation, we applied and edited Materials and Physics Components. We have accomplished quite a lot but it has all been groundwork. In this chapter, we completed steps one through four of the Mecanim workflow. In the next chapter, we will execute the creation of a Mecanim state machine and get our cyborgNinja going.

CHAPTER 34

Mecanim Execution

I N THE PREVIOUS CHAPTER, we took great pains to prepare Mecanim for use. In this chapter, we will create the state machine that will drive cyborgNinja's animations.

The fact that we have cyborgNinja@run in Scene suggests that we also have the run animation in the Scene as well. Extrapolating this assumption would suggest that you get other animations into the Scene by dragging and dropping them. This is not actually the case. The name cyborgNinja@ run is misleading. Note that if we expand cyborgNinja@run in Scene View, the run animation element is missing. It has been left behind in Assets. It is worth repeating that, conceptually, imported animation file Assets are poorly constructed contraptions. **Animations are added to the Scene/GameObject as Motions ("Animations" was taken by Unity's legacy system) in the Animator Controller (state machine).**

- Open the previous Scene, **Save Scene as... sec3Chap34Mecanim ExecutionPractice**.

- In **Scene View**, rename **cyborgNinja@Run** to **cyborgNinjaModel**.

- With the mouse cursor in the Animator View, right-click and select **Create State>Empty**.

- A **State** is created (yellow signifies that it is the Start State).

- In the **Inspector View**, rename New State to **run**.

- Click the selection target icon and with the **Assets** tab active, specify the animation **run** (Unity comes with a run animation; select the second run) as the **Motion**.

- Create a second **Camera** in the Scene View and position it to face cyborgNinjaModel.

- Change Camera's layer to **Main Camera**; change Main Camera's layer to **Untagged**.

- Hit Play.

- Note that the cyborgNinjaModel only runs briefly.

The Ninja goes, but we want it to go Ninja, go Ninja, go—that is, repeatedly, looping. Only a minimum of animation attributes can be edited in the Animator and looping is not one of them. It cannot be looped in the State. Animations are a little like prefabs. The Asset must be edited and then each instance will update throughout Animators.

- Select the **cyborgNinja@run Asset**.

- Activate **Animations** in the **Control Bar** (Figure 34.1).

- Check **Loop Time**.

- Hit **Play**.

- In the Warning Window that appears, hit **Apply**.

- CyborgNinja is up and running.

Now that CyborgNinja runs, let's enable his attack and hit animations. We will need to add additional states.

- Right-click in the **Animator** grid and choose **Create State>Empty**.

- Repeat.

- Select one **State** and in the Inspector, name it **attack**.

- Select the other State and in the Inspector, name it **hit**.

- Right-click State run and select **Make Transition**; drag the **Transition** into State attack.

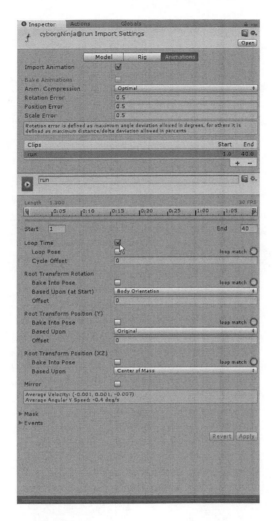

FIGURE 34.1   The Animation's Inspector with Loop Time being checked.

- Right-click State run and select Make Transition; drag the Transition into State hit.

- In State attack, specify the **Motion** as attack.

- In State hit, specify the **Motion** as hit.

In PlayMaker's Graph View, Transitions are comprised of a State addendum and a Link arrow. Transitional Events per se are not edited; they are simply specified as jumping-off points for conditionals. **In Mecanim, the Transitions themselves are selected and edited in the Inspector View.**

Transitions only have one type of instruction (aka Action): Conditions. Conditions are decided by one of four Parameters: Float, Int, Bool, and Trigger.

Other than these distinctions, the state machine philosophy remains the same. Everything in a finite state machine exists in a State. Within a State, Actions (aka instructions) are performed. Some Actions store their results as Variables. Other Actions, known as conditionals, check for a particular *change* in a Variable. If it exists, the conditional causes a Transition (aka Transitional Event) from one State to another. Let's edit the pathways to facilitate movement and change.

- In the lower left-hand corner of the **Animator View**, click the + symbol next to **Parameters**.

- Select **Bool** and name it **attacking**.

- Repeat and name the second Bool **hitting**.

- Click the **Transition** that leads into **attack**.

- In the **Inspector View**, in **Conditions**, select **attacking**.

- Ensure **true** is the Bool (Figure 34.2).

- Select the Transition that leads into **hit**.

FIGURE 34.2   Here we see the Animator and Transitions Inspector View properly edited.

- In the Inspector View, in Conditions, select hitting.

- Select true as the Bool.

- Your Animator is complete!

This is nearly as simple as an Animator can be. Simplicity results from proper planning, which traces back to a properly pruned design document.

In part, because our example is so simple, the advantages of Mecanim may not be readily apparent. Why use Mecanim instead of PlayMaker and Unity's legacy (previous) animation system? One reason to use Mecanim is its ability to blend animations. **Avatar Masks and (Animator Controller) Layers allow you to mix and match animations. Much like adding multiple FSMs to a single GameObject, you can add multiple Layers to an Animator Controller. Multiple Layers can work simultaneously; one blends with or overrides the other**. This is efficient. Instead of having an idle, an idle and shooting, a walking, a walking and shooting, a running, a running and shooting, a jumping, and a jumping and shooting animation, you can simply have an idle, walk, run, jump, and shoot animation. Using an Avatar Mask, you can then specify that the shoot animation only has an effect on the arms allowing you to mix and match "shoot" with the other animations. In the latter instance, the animator (the person, not the Unity system of the same name) needs only to create five animations instead of eight. The more animations, the greater the efficiencies provided by Avatar Masks and Layers. In the interests of course completion, let's briefly look at the creation of Avatar Masks and Layers.

- In **Assets>Models>cyborgNinja**, right-click and select **Create>Avatar Mask** and name it **armsOnlyAvatarMask**.

- In the Inspector View, expand **Humanoid** and deactivate everything but the arms by clicking everything but the arms and their children (Figure 34.3).

- In the upper left-hand corner of the **Animator View**, click the + next to **Layers**.

- Name the Layer the **armsOnlyLayer**.

- Note that similar to the addition of a new FSM to a GameObject, a new Layer creates a new and empty state machine Graph View.

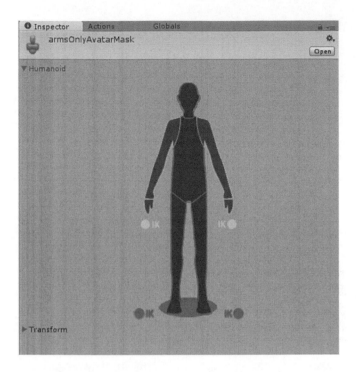

FIGURE 34.3   Here is a Humanoid image with everything deactivated but the arms.

- Turn the **Weight** parameter up to 1 (possibly unnecessary with Override selected).

- Note that in some Unity versions, the Avatar Mask cannot be dragged and dropped into the **Mask** field but don't panic; click the selection target icon and select armsOnlyAvatarMask (Figure 34.4).

FIGURE 34.4   The Animator View with the newly created armsOnlyLayer edited as described earlier.

This is the extent of our Avatar Mask and Layers lesson. Completion of the armsOnlyLayer would involve the creation of a state machine in the Animator View complete with State(s), Motions, and potentially, Transitions. When triggered by PlayMaker, the (arm) animations in the armsOnlyLayer would then override the (arm) animations in the default Base Layer according to what has been specified in the armsOnlyAvatarMask (in this case, the arms). Thus, it is seen that Avatar Masks and (Animator Controller) Layers allow you to mix and match animations thereby obtaining efficiency.

In Unity 5, Parameters occupy a separate tab and can also be accessed from a separate Animator Parameter View. An Animator comes with two additional States: **Entry** and **Exit,** which, in our instructions, are ignored. Entry is assumed to be much like the Start Transition of PlayMaker. Exit can be bypassed.

In this chapter, we applied our knowledge of PlayMaker to Mecanim. We created a fully functional Animator. We also took a look at (Animator Controller) Layers and Avatar Masks to see how to efficiently mix and match animations. In the next chapter, we will integrate PlayMaker with our Animator. Spoiler alert: There will be troubleshooting.

CHAPTER 35

Mecanim–PlayMaker Integration and Artificial Intelligence

W E WILL BUILD SOME rudimentary cyborgNinja AI (chase humans, kill all humans) in this chapter. As we progress, we will assign the PlayMaker Actions necessary to trigger the Parameters residing in cyborgNinjaAnimatorController (Mecanim). We will get ourselves into trouble and then reason our way out of it.

Our cyborgNinja's AI is going to be of the most simple, bug-like variety: go to food; eat food. In cyborgNinja terms, that translates as "go to human, slice human into thirds with katana."

- Open the previous Scene, **Save Scene as... sec3Chap35Mecanim PlayMakerIntegrationPractice**.

- Select the **cyborgNinjaModel** and in PlayMaker View, right-click to add **FSM**; name it **AI**.

- Rename the first State **goTo**.

- Add a **Smooth Look At Action** and specify the **fpsCharStandIn** as the Target Object.

- Add a **Move Towards** Action and specify the fpsCharStandIn as the **Target Object**.

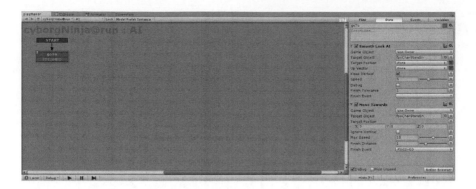

FIGURE 35.1   The goTo State and its necessary Actions.

- In the PlayMaker Graph View, right-click the goTo State and **Add Transition Finished**.

- Specify the **Finish Distance** as 1 and the **Finish Event** as **FINISHED** (Figure 35.1).

- Add a new state named **attack**.

- In the attack State, simply add the Action **Set Animator Bool** and type in **attacking** for the **Parameter**.

- Check the **Value** parameter so that attacking will be set to true (Figure 35.2).

- Copy the Set Animator Bool Action.

- In the goTo State, highlight the Smooth Look At Action, right-click, and select **Paste Actions Before**.

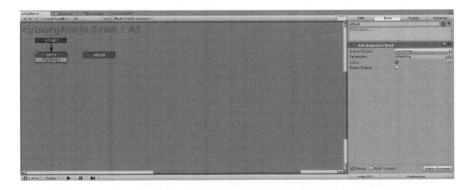

FIGURE 35.2   Pictured here is the attack State and its necessary Actions.

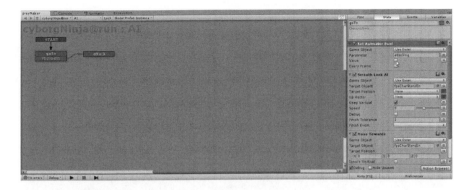

FIGURE 35.3 The FSM thus far with the goTo State selected and the Set Animator Bool properly specified.

- Uncheck Set Animator Bool's Value parameter (sometimes variables will get stuck in a value that persists despite Play restarts; this makes sure the attacking parameter is properly initialized as false).

- Drag a Transition link from FINISHED to attack (Figure 35.3).

To test our AI and accompanying animations, we will have to edit our cameras and randomSpawner FSM. We will deactivate Camera and redesignate Main Camera's layer. Then, we will delete our cyborgNinjaStandIn and properly specify cyborgNinjaModel in the previously mentioned FSM's randomSpawning State.

- Deactivate **Camera**.

- Select **Main Camera** and redesignate its **Layer** as **Main Camera**.

- Temporarily move **cyborgNinjaModel** closer to and more or less level with **fpsCharStandIn**.

- Hit **Play** and observe in Scene View.

The cyborgNinja attacks! Running, however, seems to be a problem. Also, he is floating in the air. That's not good.

35.1 TROUBLESHOOTING

Once again, one of Unity's killer features is its allowance for real-time editing. That will help us quickly pare down the number of culprits that may be responsible for the run animation fail.

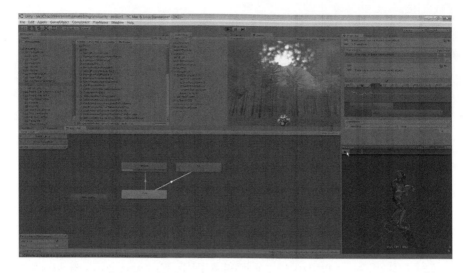

FIGURE 35.4 With the Transition selected we can see the mouse cursor activating the Preview animation in the Inspector View.

- Hit **Play**.

- In **Animator View**, click the **Transition** between **run** and **attack States** and expand and play the **Preview** animation (Figure 35.4).

- Note that the cyborgNinja is not running in the Preview animation either.

- Right-click the attack State and choose **Delete**.

- Note that cyborgNinja now runs properly.

- Exit **Game Mode**.

From this experiment, we can conclude that run *can* still work, just not in conjunction with attack. **When one thing works and a seemingly similar other thing does not, it is best to scrutinize them for differences.** Since run was working before the introduction of attack, we will assume that attack is the culprit and examine it first.

- In **Assets>Models>cyborgNinja** select **cyborgNinja@attack**.

- Select **Rig**.

- Note that its Animation type is erroneously set to **Generic**, not **Humanoid**.

- Correct the oversight.

- Its **Avatar Definition** specification should be **Copy From Other Avatar**.

- Recalling that **Avatars** (skeletal system translation files) can be used across multiple **Models**, specify the **Source** parameter as **cyborg Ninja@runAvatar**.

- Hit **Apply** (and **Update** if necessary).

- Repeat any and all steps necessary to ensure that **cyborgNinja@hit** is likewise correctly configured.

- Hit **Play**.

- CyborgNinja runs, attacks, and does everything.

There is still a problem. CyborgNinja is floating in the air like a lethargic helium balloon. The Move To Action in the cyborgNinja's AI FSM is calculating from its pivot point, which is currently located at the Model's feet. As was alluded to in a previous chapter, we will have to use a pivot point hack to make CyborgNinja's movement more convincing.

- Create an empty GameObject named **cyborgNinjaPivotPoint**.

- Position it so that it is more or less center of mass of the **cyborgNinja** mesh (Figure 35.5).

- Child **cyborgNinjaModel** to cyborgNinjaPivotPoint.

- With cyborgNinjaModel's **goTo** State selected, specify the **Move Towards** Action's **GameObject** as **Specify GameObject**.

- In the resulting field, specify cyborgNinjaPivotPoint.

- Hit **Play** and observe.

- Note that it may take repeated playtesting, unchilding, repositioning, and rechilding to correctly determine the best possible position of cyborgNinjaPivotPoint.

Things are going great! While we are here and on a roll, let's round out the AI FSM. We may not always be able to anticipate everything we need in an FSM. Often, we will need to revisit and update FSMs as messages

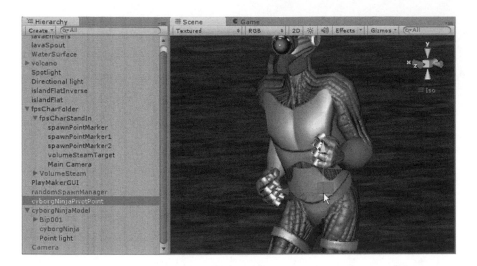

FIGURE 35.5 The cyborgNinjaPivotPoint (represented by the Transform Gizmo) positioned so that it is more or less the center of mass of the cyborgNinja mesh.

get sent back and forth and their interconnectedness increases. We can, however, anticipate the need to short-circuit the AI's attack logic if cyborgNinja gets hit. In that instance, PlayMaker should tell Mecanim to play cyborgNinja's hit animation. PlayMaker should then wait a moment and afterward reset Mecanim's Bool Parameter.

- In the **AI** FSM, with **Events** active in the Control Bar, **Add Event toHit**.

- Make it Global (check the box next to its name).

- In Graph View, add the State **hit**.

- Right-click State hit and **Add Global Transition** toHit.

- Add Action **Set Animator Bool**.

- Specify **Parameter** as **hitting**.

- Check mark **Value**.

- Add Action **Wait**; set the **Time** to 2.

- Right-click State hit and Add Transition **FINISHED**.

- Specify Action Wait's **Finish Event** as FINISHED.

- In the AI's Graph View, add the State **reset**.

- In State hit, right-click Set Animator Bool and **Copy Selected Actions**.

- Add the Set Animator Bool Action to State reset by right-clicking and choosing **Paste Actions**.

- Uncheck Value.

It is probably not a bad idea to deactivate cyborgNinja here in this state. The reason is that transition into this State is the result of a hard-coded parameter in the previous Wait Action. The parameter corresponds to the length of the hit animation. If we deactivate cyborgNinja from a different State in a different FSM, it might necessitate a synchronous Wait Action with the same hard-coded value. If that value were to change, we would need to remember to update it by hand in two places instead of one. Alternately, we could use variables of course, but that seems needlessly complicated. To keep costs down, we will deactivate the cyborgNinja here in the reset State.

- Add Action **Activate GameObject**.

- In **GameObject**, select **Specify GameObject**.

- Drag and drop **cyborgNinjaPivotPoint** into the resulting field.

- Uncheck the box next to **Activate**.

- Drag a Transition Link from State hit's FINISHED Transition to State reset (Figure 35.6).

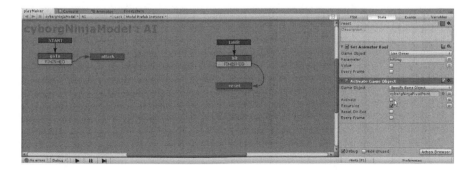

FIGURE 35.6 Shown here, the AI FSM thus far with the reset State selected and its Action visible.

In this chapter, we learned that Mecanim–PlayMaker Integration is as simple as using PlayMaker Animator Proxy Actions to tell the Animator Parameters what they should be (e.g., attacking = true). We also added +5 to our troubleshooting skills and have working AI. In the next chapter, we will solidify our Mecanim knowledge and abilities by constructing an Animator for our player's character Model.

CHAPTER 36

FPS Character Model's Mecanim

W E WILL REVIEW OUR Mecanim workflow as we get our fpsChar-Model working. We will integrate PlayMaker and do some more troubleshooting in this chapter.

- Open the previous scene, **Save Scene as... sec3Chap36fpsCharacter MecanimPractice**.

- Import **fpsCharArms@Shooting** into a new **fpsChar** folder in **Assets>Models**.

- Note that since this is not a bipedal Humanoid, it can use a **Generic Animation Type** as specified in **Rig**.

- Child fpsCharArms@Shooting to **fpsCharFolder** and specify its **Scale** as 3.5, 3.5, 3.5.

- Position fpsCharArms@Shooting so that the Main Camera can clearly see the hands and some of the arms.

- Select all **fpsCharStandIn** children and assign them as children to fpsCharArms@Shooting instead.

- Delete fpsCharStandIn.

- Rename fpsCharArms@Shooting to **fpsCharModel**.

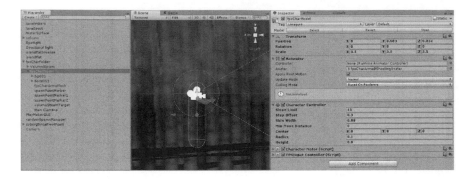

FIGURE 36.1 The results of the importation and parenting process of fpsCharModel.

- Add the **FPSInput Controller** Component and **Mouse Look** Component to fpsCharModel.

- Edit the **Character Controller** Component so that the associated Collider does not clip through **islandFlat** (Figure 36.1).

- In **Assets>Models>fpsChar**, create an **Animator Controller** and name it **fpsCharAnimatorController**.

- In the **Animator** Component in fpsCharModel's **Inspector View**, specify fpsCharAnimatorController as the **Controller**.

- While making sure that fpsCharAnimatorController is selected, right-click and add a state in the Animator View; name it **idle**.

- Specify its **Motion** as **Idle** (the first Idle).

- Right-click to add state **shoot**.

- Specify its Motion as **Shooting**.

- Create **Parameter shooting**; declare it to be a **Bool**.

- Right-click on state idle and select **Make Transition**.

- Drag the **transition** into state shoot.

- Click the transition and specify its **Conditions** as **shooting true**.

In our cyborgNinjaAnimatorController, the hit and attack states were both dead ends. The attack state is a dead end quite literally; the player's character is dead and the game is over. If the hit state is activated, it means that the cyborgNinja has been shot and it will deactivate. In either case, the cyborgNinja need not be animated anymore. With fpsCharModel, however, after it is done shooting, it should return to its **Idle** animation.

- Right-click on state **shoot** and select **Make Transition**.

- Drag the transition into state **idle**.

- Click the transition and note that its **Exit Time**, the default **Condition**, is equal to the length of the shooting animation, .88 seconds.

36.1 TROUBLESHOOTING

It may appear as if this is all we need. However, playtesting would reveal that the fpsCharModel will not always shoot on command. This is because an **Exit Time** transition is essentially limbo. That is to say, there is no way to transition out of a transition; you are stuck in it for as long as the transition takes. A Bool switch is instantaneous so you are never stuck in it for long; in the **shoot → Idle** transition, however, we are stuck for .88 seconds. Because shooting a cyborgNinja is a life and death matter, .88 seconds seems like an eternity. Our fpsChar needs to shoot and shoot some more, pronto. The simplest solution is to construct our controller so that the fpsChar has the option to transition not only into idle but into additional shooting.

- Right-click on the **shoot** state.

- Select **Copy**.

- In the negative space of the **Animator Controller** "Graph View," right-click and select **Paste**.

- Right-click in the shoot state and select **Make Transition**.

- Drag the transition into the **shoot 0** state.

- Click the transition and specify its **Conditions** as **shooting true**.

- Right-click in the shoot 0 state and select Make Transition.

- Drag the transition into the shoot state.

- Click the transition and specify its Conditions as shooting true.

- Right-click in the shoot 0 state and select Make Transition.

- Drag the transition into the **idle** state (Figure 36.2).

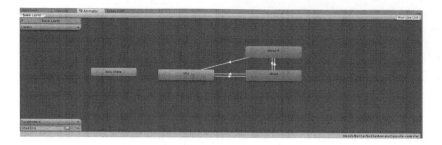

FIGURE 36.2   The completed fpsCharAnimatorController.

There is still the potential for the Char to be stranded in the shoot → Idle transition but it is minimal. There is a bigger problem we have to worry about now; fpsChar can shoot plenty but not plenty fast enough. That is the result of Unity's default animation blending. Typically, the default blending settings are fine. Blending allows animation transitions to look natural. But when your life is on the line, you don't want natural; you want Bob Munden fast.

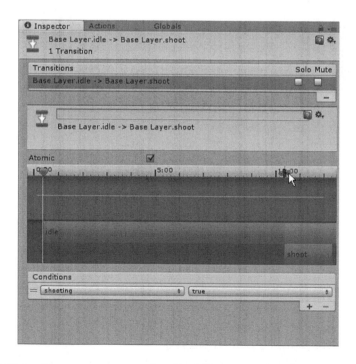

FIGURE 36.3   Here we see a properly edited Transition Timeline.

- Click on the **transition** that leads from state **idle** into state **shoot**.

- In the Transition **Timeline,** select the rightmost slider marker.

- Move the rightmost slider marker to the left until the space between it and the left slider marker is eliminated (in this instance the percentage should be 50%).

- Note that the blue tint representing the blend time has likewise been eliminated (Figure 36.3).

- Repeat the process above with all the transitions that lead into a shoot state.

- Shooting has itself been shot; troubleshoot, that is.

In Unity 5, there have been some changes made to transitions. It now appears as if you can potentially interrupt and exit a transition.

We have created an Animator Controller for our newly imported fpsCharModel and further solidified our understanding of Mecanim. We troubleshoot until the Animator Controller was sure to work satisfactorily. It will fire rapidly and successively thanks in part to our newly acquired blend editing know-how. In the next chapter, we will integrate the fpsCharAnimatorController with its associated PlayMaker FSM.

CHAPTER 37

FPS Character Model's Mecanim–PlayMaker Integration

I N THIS CHAPTER, WE will create an FSM with Actions that tell the Animation Controller Parameters what to be and do. This will conclude our review of Mecanim. With the time remaining, we will get some odds and ends taken care of.

- Open the previous scene, **Save Scene as… sec3Chap37fpsCharacter MecanimPlayMakerIntegrationPractice**.

- Select **fpsCharModel**.

- In the PlayMaker Graph View, right-click to add FSM **firing**.

- With **Event** activated in the Control Bar, **Add Event "toFire."**

- Rename the first State as **ready**.

- With **State** activated in the Control Bar, add action **Set Animator Bool** and **Get Mouse Button Down**.

- In Set Animator Bool, specify **Parameter** as **shooting**, and ensure **Value** is unchecked.

- In Get Mouse Button Down, specify **Send Event** as **toFire**.

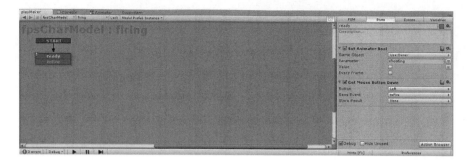

FIGURE 37.1 PlayMaker View with the ready State selected and State activated in the Control Bar with its actions properly configured.

- In the Graph View, right-click State ready and **Add Transition** toFire (Figure 37.1).

- Right-click in the Graph View and **Add State** "**fire**."

- With State fire selected and State activated in the Control Bar, add action Set Animator Bool and **Next Frame Event**.

- In Set Animator Bool, specify Parameter as "shooting" and ensure Value is checked.

- In the Graph View, right-click State fire and **Add Transition FINISHED**.

- In Next Frame Event, specify **Send Event** as FINISHED.

- Drag transition **links** from one State to the next creating a closed loop (Figure 37.2).

- Our fpsCharModel can now mime shoot.

While we are here and have some extra time, let's add our gunshot sound effect. Obviously, in a perfect world, the Audio Source would be attached to the gun, but the arms are spatially near enough that the end user will not be able to discern any fault. Adding it here will save us from having to create an additional FSM.

- Select **fpsCharModel**; in the firing FSM, select the **fire** State.

- Add action **Audio Play** to the top of the queue.

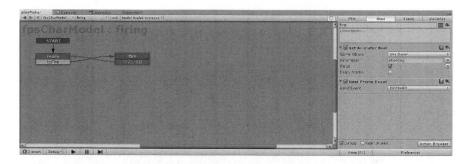

FIGURE 37.2   The PlayMaker View with the fire State selected and activated in the Control Bar with its actions properly configured.

- Follow the on-screen instructions and **Click to Add Required Component**.

- Select and hold and then drag and drop a downloaded and imported gunshot sound effect into the **One Shot Clip** field.

- In the **Audio Source** component, uncheck **Play On Awake**.

- Note that the **Audio Clip** field need not be specified; completion of the Audio Play action is sufficient.

It seems as if we are progressing by leaps and bounds. Let's texture our arms.

- Into **Assets>Textures**, import **fpsCharArmsDiff.jpg** and **fpsCharArmsNormals.jpg**.

- Select and hold and then drag and drop **fpsCharArmsDiff** onto **fpsCharArmsMesh** in the Hierarchy View (expand fpsCharFolder if necessary).

- In the Inspector View, specify **Shader** as **Bumped Specular**.

- Add fpsCharArmsNormals to the Normalmap slot; click "Fix Now."

- Select **fpsCharFolder** and add a **Point light**; position it just above the fpsCharModel's arms.

- Dial its **Range** down to 2.

- Select fpsCharArmsMesh and in the Inspector View; **Add Layer... fpsChar**.

FIGURE 37.3   Our sweater-wearing arms textured and lit.

- Reselect fpsCharArmsMesh and in the Inspector View specify **layer** as fpsChar.

- Select the newly created Point light and specify that its **Culling Mask** is nothing other than fpsChar.

- Set **Render Mode** as **Important** (Figure 37.3).

- Hit **Play**.

- If unsatisfied with the arms, play with the **Scale** of fpsCharModel and the **Position** of Main Camera.

- Note that even without a gun, our arms are so convincing and menacing that cyborgNinja backpedals for its life (we will correct this later).

Finally, we need to account for the possibility that the cyborgNinja will defeat the player and the game will end. In that event, we want the player to no longer be able to mime shooting. Presumably, the avatar will be dead:

- With **Events** active in the PlayMaker Control Bar, **Add Event "toGameOver."**

- Mark the box next to its name to make it global.

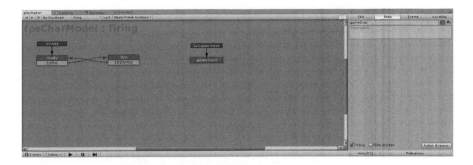

FIGURE 37.4   Pictured here is the firing FSM complete with dead end.

- Right-click in the PlayMaker Graph View to Add State "gameOver."

- Right-click State gameOver and **Add Global Transition** toGameOver (Figure 37.4).

The majority of Mecanim work is preparation work. Once again, PlayMaker-Mecanim integration is as simple as adding PlayMaker Actions that tell the Animator Controller Parameters what to be and do. Currently, however, the fpsCharModel is only miming the act of shooting. To calculate whether or not bullets will successfully intercept the cyborgNinja, we will have to use an action known as **Raycast**. In the next chapter, Raycasting will be discussed.

CHAPTER 38

Raycasting

R AYCASTING IS A COMMON and useful Action. In this chapter, we will create a **Raycast** Action to check if, when our player shoots, the "bullets" intercept the cyborgNinja GameObject. If the ray does connect, we will send a message to cyborgNinja informing it that it has been hit. Previously, we learned to receive messages using Global Transitions. To send messages from FSMs, we will learn to use the **Send Event** action. Upon receipt, cyborgNinja will then know to play its hit animation, wait, and deactivate according to our earlier instructions. When things go wrong, we will have to troubleshoot.

Raycasting is just what it sounds like, casting a ray. It is the act of using math to draw a line out from a point of origin. This is done to see what, if anything, the line intersects. Typical uses include calculating line of sight and projectile paths. We will be using it for the latter. Since our Raycast FSM mimics shooting, it will, in places, resemble the State machine from the previous lesson (Figure 38.1). Let's begin.

- Open the previous scene, **Save Scene as… sec3Chap38Raycasting**.

- Create an **empty GameObject "raygun"** and child it to **fpsCharModel**.

- Position raygun so that it is out in front of where a gun would be held when aimed.

- In the PlayMaker Graph View, right-click to add FSM **RaycastingBullets**.

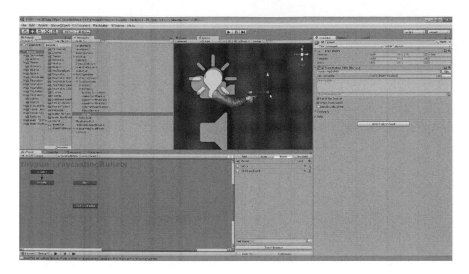

FIGURE 38.1   The scene edits thus far.

- Rename the first State as **ready**.

- In the Graph View, right-click and **Add State** "**fire**."

- Repeat creating State **hitSendEvent**.

- With **Event** activated in the Control Bar, **Add Event** "**toFire**" and Add Event **toHitSendEvent** (Figure 38.1).

- Select the ready State; add the Action **Get Mouse Button Down**.

- Specify **Send Event** as **toFire**.

- In the Graph View, right-click State ready, and **Add Transition** toFire.

- Click the fire State and in the Control Bar, activate State; add the Action **Raycast**.

Raycast has many settings. Currently, we are only interested in finding out what the Raycast intercepts and if that thing is the cyborgNinja. We will store what the Raycast hits as a GameObject variable. Then in a second Action, we will compare the variable against the cyborgNinja GameObject and instruct what should happen if they match. The first step is creating the GameObject variable.

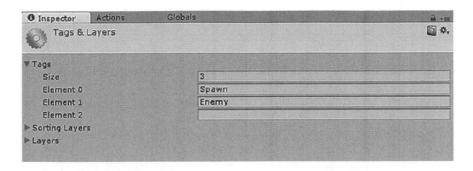

FIGURE 38.2   Here we see properly configured Tags & Layers fields.

- In the Control Bar, activate **Variables**.

- In the **New Variable** field, type **hitObject** and specify its **Variable Type** as **GameObject**.

- Click **Add**.

- Check the box next to **Inspector**.

- Back in the Raycast Action, set **Store Hit Object** to **hitObject**.

- Check **Debug**.

- Add the Action **GameObject Compare Tag**.

- Specify **GameObject*** as **hitObject**.

- In the **Tag** rollout, select **Add Tag**.

- In the **Inspector View**, type **Enemy** into the **Element 1** field (Figure 38.2).

- Back in the GameObject Compare Tag Action, set Tag as Enemy.

- In the Graph View, right-click State fire, **Add Transition toHitSend-Event** and Add Transition FINISHED.

- Specify GameObject Compare Tag's **True Event** as **toHitSendEvent** and **False Event** as **FINISHED** (Figure 38.3).

Understand that we are not comparing GameObject directly; we are only able to compare against a GameObject's tag. Obviously, the FSM will not work unless the game object that we want to test as having been hit actually has the Enemy tag.

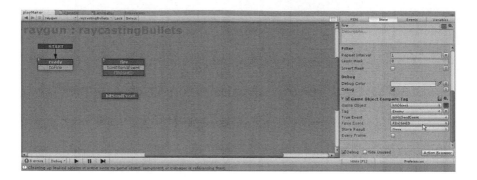

FIGURE 38.3   A proper fire State (portions of Action Raycast are obscured).

- In the Hierarchy View, select **cyborgNinjaModel**.

- At the top of the Inspector View, set its **Tag** to **Enemy**.

If the **fire** State determines that cyborgNinjaModel has been shot, then we will inform it of its wounding in the **hitSendEvent** State (Figure 38.4). Recall that we anticipated this possibility and have already set up a toHit Global Transition in the AI FSM with which to receive our message.

- In the **Hierarchy View**, choose **raygun**.

- Select the **hitSendEvent** State.

- Add the Action **Send Event**.

- **Event Target** is **GameObject FSM**.

FIGURE 38.4   Pictured here is a properly configured hitSendEvent State.

- Set **GameObject** to **Specify GameObject**.

- Drag **cyborgNinjaModel** into the resulting field.

- Select **AI** for the **FSM Name**.

- Choose **toHit** for **Send Event***.

- Add Action **Next Frame Event**.

- Specify **Send Event** as **FINISHED**.

- Right-click State **hitSendEvent** and **Add Transition FINISHED** (Figure 38.4).

Chief among the repercussions of the cyborgNinja being hit is that the cyborgNinja must deactivate and the randomSpawner must restart. It is necessary to restart FSM randomSpawner so that the cyborgNinja has reoccurring opportunities to ambush the player. It is possible to Send Event from here, but note that in doing so, we would be activating randomSpawner for a full 2 seconds before cyborgNinja even deactivates. That is because the AI FSM had been given a Wait Action to allow the hit animation time to play. Since it takes at least 5 seconds for the cyborgNinja to repawn, we would still have 3 seconds of leeway. If either randomSpawner's Random Float Action parameters or AI's Wait Action's parameters were to change however, problems would arise. Bottom line is that it is best to make sure that we don't restart randomSpawner until after (or *immediately* before) cyborgNinja deactivates.

- Right-click **Send Event** and choose **Copy Selected Actions**.

- Select **cyborgNinjaModel**.

- In the **AI** FSM, select State **reset**.

- Right-click and **Paste Actions**.

- Ensure that the newly pasted Send Event is *immediately* before **Activate GameObject** in the Event's queue (by dragging it if necessary).

- As in the previous Send Event, **Event Target** is **GameObject FSM**.

- **GameObject** is **Specify GameObject**.

- Drag **randomSpawnManager** into the resulting field.

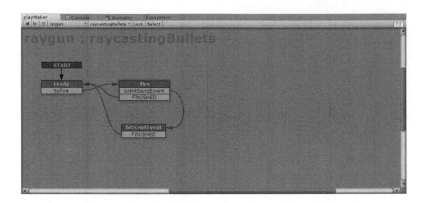

FIGURE 38.5   The links between States.

- Select **randomSpawner** for the **FSM Name**.

- Choose **restart** for **Send Event**.

We need to link up the States in RaycastingBullets. By now, you are sure to understand how to wire States with Transitional Links.

- Select **raygun** and in **RaycastingBullets**, link the States in a logical manner.

- If you encounter problems, refer to Figure 38.5.

Finally, as in the previous chapter, we need to account for the possibility that the cyborgNinja will defeat the player and the game will end. In that event, we want the player to no longer be able to Raycast.

- With **Events** active in the PlayMaker Control Bar, **Add Event** "**toGameOver**."

- Mark the box next to its name to make it global.

- Right-click in the PlayMaker Graph View to Add State "gameOver."

- Right-click State gameOver and **Add Global Transition** toGameOver (Figure 38.6).

Raycasting can be fraught. It will require playtesting.

- Temporarily dock Scene View side by side with Play View.

- Hit **Play**.

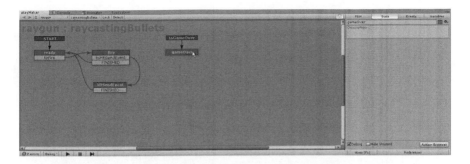

FIGURE 38.6   RaycastingBullets FSM complete with dead end.

- Observe the Scene View and **RaycastingBullets** FSM while firing (left mouse button).

- Note that nothing works.

- Exit Play Mode.

38.1 TROUBLESHOOTING

Examination of our FSM while playing elicits the fact that we never move past the fire State. In this State, there are only two Actions that can possibly be misconfigured. Assuming that cyborgNinjaModel has been given the tag Enemy, the error is most likely in the more complicated of the two Actions: Raycast. Having enabled the Debug parameter, the ray should appear in Scene View as a bright yellow line. Visual confirmation will assist in our troubleshooting efforts.

- Hit **Play**.

- Again, observe the Scene View and **RaycastingBullets** FSM while firing.

- Note the absence of a bright yellow **Debug** line.

- Exit Play Mode.

The line is not there, which indicates that Action Raycast is not Raycasting. Believe it or not, the default setting of Raycast is *not* to Raycast. It is currently specified to Raycast in *no* direction; we must specify that it Raycasts in *a* direction.

- In Action **Raycast**, expand the **Direction** parameter (depress the list icon).

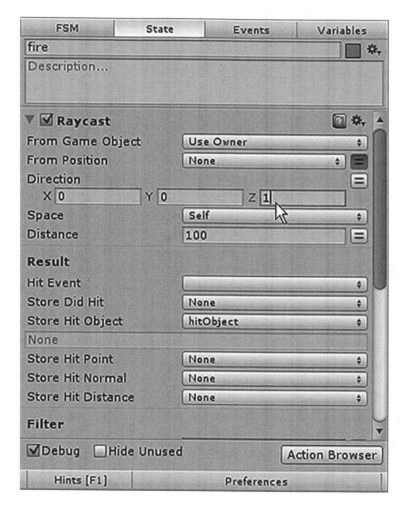

FIGURE 38.7   Raycast's Direction parameter is shown here properly edited.

- Set **Z** as 1 (Figure 38.7).

- Hit **Play**.

- Again, observe the Scene View and **RaycastingBullets** FSM while firing.

- Note the appearance of a bright yellow **Debug** line.

- You are now Raycasting.

- Exit Play Mode.

There is still a problem in this FSM and it is much more difficult to troubleshoot. Most problems self-evince by prohibiting what is intended to happen from happening. That is to say, what we want and expect to happen does not happen. A more insidious bug results in the opposite; what we want and expect to happen *does* happen but for the wrong reasons.

Here is what's happening; if the player successfully shoots the cyborg-Ninja, most of everything that is intended to happen does happen, including the GameObject cyborgNinjaModel being stored in the hitObject GameObject variable. The problem is that cyborgNinjaModel *continues* to be stored in the hitObject GameObject variable. If nothing supplants this value, it means that the cyborgNinjaModel will deactivate with every subsequent left-click of the mouse. The developer might attribute the results to having very, very good aim and never properly identify the bug!

It is important, therefore, to always reinitialize variables. In this case, the hitObject GameObject variable needs to be reset as false.

- Select State **ready**.

- Add the Action **Set GameObject**.

- Specify **Variable** as **hitObject** and **GameObject** as **None (GameObject)**.

In this chapter, we learned the reasons for and how to Raycast. We facilitated interconnectedness by using the Action Send Event, thereby expanding our game's ability (and complexity) nigh exponentially. We troubleshot the most common Raycast error: failure to specify Direction. In addition to bad things happening, good things happening for the wrong reasons also constitute bugs. We learned to always reinitialize our variables.

CHAPTER 39

The User Interface

I**N THIS CHAPTER, WE** will learn to create graphical user interface elements. We will make several buttons with which the player can control
the game software. We will also configure the UI to accommodate multiple screen resolutions.

**GUI, of course, stands for graphical user interface. For the most
part, the purpose of a GUI in a game is to allow the player to control
the game software directly rather than through an in-game avatar.
Typically, a GUI is made up of icons and text that can be clicked, slid,
typed, or dragged and dropped. Buttons, sliders, and text fields are
all examples of GUI elements.** In Unity, GUI refers to a legacy system.
**The newest implementation of its graphical user interface is referred
to as UI.**

**Think of the most common type of UI as utilizing a transparent
overlay. It renders over the top everything else in the scene. On the
transparent overlay, which in Unity is called the Canvas, icons and text
are drawn.**

As with Mecanim, you could dedicate a small book to Unity's UI system. However, to ship our game on time, we really only need to learn and
do three things:

1. Get UI elements into the scene.

2. Configure and position them.

3. Texture them.

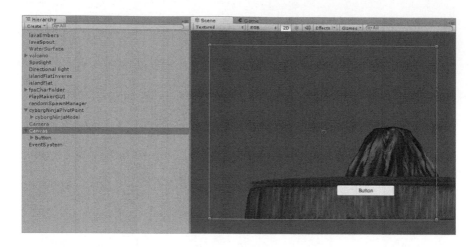

FIGURE 39.1 The Canvas/Button pair in the Hierarchy View as well as its representation in Scene View.

Let's begin by putting a **Button** UI element in the scene. Note that without anything selected in the hierarchy, **Component>UI>Button** is inaccessible. We will need to bypass the Main Menu Bar (Figure 39.1).

- Open the previous scene, **Save Scene as… sec3Chap39UIPractice**.

- In the **Hierarchy View**, right-click and select **UI>Button**.

- In the **Scene View** Control Bar, click **2D**.

- Press hotkey **F** to center the newly created **Button**.

- Note that as the Button was created, **Canvas** and **EventSystem** were created concurrently.

- In the Hierarchy View, select Canvas.

- In the Scene View, press hotkey F to center the newly created Canvas.

- Zoom in (using the mouse scroll wheel button) if necessary.

- Note that it is represented by a white border and four blue vertices (Figure 39.1).

In the **Canvas** component, there is a **Render Mode** drop-down that elicits three choices. We will only be working with **Screen Space—Overlay** but in the interest of course completion, you should learn about all three.

1. **Screen Space—Overlay**: This is the most common type of Canvas. It is simply a transparent overlay. It and its UI elements render on top of everything else in the scene.

2. **Screen Space—Camera**: This is much like Screen Space—Overlay except that it is rendered as if it were on a plane a set distance from its camera. The plane can be tilted as well, thereby achieving foreshortening effects.

3. **World Space**: Allows you to establish a Canvas as if it is a GameObject. Rather than always being a set distance from the camera, the Canvas can be positioned "physically" in the scene. An example use case would be the UI system for an in-game cell phone.

The Scene View representation of our Screen Space—Overlay Canvas is completely arbitrary. It looks as if it is measured in Unity units and has positional coordinates that place it "physically" in the scene. Neither is true. It does not occupy a location in the scene; it is simply a camera overlay. For that reason, it is not measured in Unity units but rather in pixels. The Canvas' dimensions are those of your game's screen resolution.

- Temporarily undock the Game View so that it floats next to the Scene View.

- Adjust the size of the Game View.

- Note that the Scene View representation of the **Canvas** scales accordingly.

- Note too that the **Button** maintains a relative position.

- Dock the Game View and Scene Views in their original location.

Now that we have our UI element in the scene, we must learn how to position it. As always, dials abound.

- With **Button** selected, click the square icon in its **Rect Transform** component displayed in the **Inspector View**.

- An **Anchor Presets** window appears; note the matrix of squares (Figure 39.2).

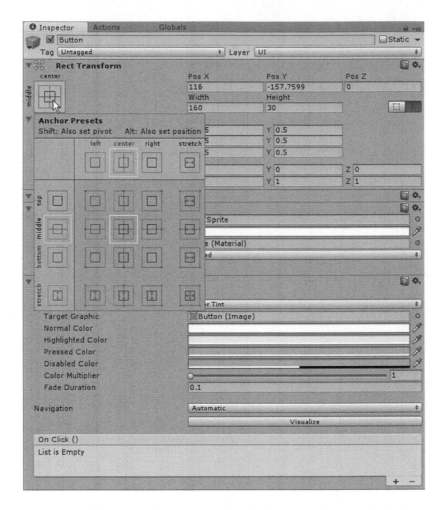

FIGURE 39.2 This is an illustration of both the square icon and the Anchor Presets window.

In the Anchor Presets window, we see a grid of squares inside squares. The outside square represents the canvas; the inside square represents our UI element. The points along the edges of the squares represent anchor positions (Figure 39.3).

In the Anchor Presets Panel, you can assign several properties to both the Canvas and the selected UI elements. You can assign the UI element the ability to stretch as the Canvas stretches (i.e., as resolution differs or changes). This is done by clicking a square icon in the outer **stretch** rows and columns. You can assign the UI an **Anchor** point. This is done by selecting any of the other icons. You can simultaneously

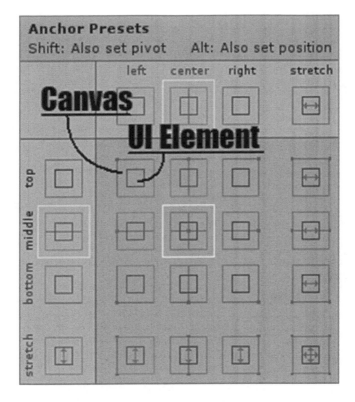

FIGURE 39.3   A diagram of the squares inside the Anchor Presets window.

define the location of the UI element's pivot point. This is accomplished by holding Shift and selecting a square from rows and columns one through three. Finally, you can move the UI element to various positions by holding the Alt key and selecting a square from those same rows and columns.

Currently, reassigning Anchors and Pivots has no discernible effect on the position of either the Canvas or UI element. What effect does the assignment of Anchors and Pivots have? Remember that as it is a child, the UI element exists in local space. Its position is relative to its parent, the Canvas. **By assigning an Anchor, you are defining the 0, 0 point of the Canvas coordinate system used to orientate the UI element. Anchors give your UI elements "stickiness." By assigning an element to an Anchor, you are defining the position to which it remains relative**.

Thereafter, Anchors and UI element Pivots are the points used when measuring to and from. With a point to measure from and a point to measure to, we can then specify the location of the UI element.

FIGURE 39.4   In the Inspector View, a padding of 20 × −20 pixels has been specified in Pos X and Pos Y; the Scene View shows these measurements as calculated
from the Anchor point (on the Canvas) to the Pivot point (on the UI element).

Positional specifications are entered into the **Pos X** and **Pos Y** fields
(Figure 39.4).

Typically, we want the button to resize and reposition according to
the end user's screen resolution. The default, oddly enough, is to resize
according to padding measured in absolute pixels. This is absurd; if the
end user has a high resolution monitor, the UI element may expand taking
up nearly the entire screen in order to maintain the specified pixel padding (Figure 39.5).

If the end user uses a small resolution, as is common of most mobile
devices, specifying absolute pixel padding may push the UI element
completely off the screen. Obviously, when designing UI for multiple
resolutions, we want to resize and reposition UI elements in terms of
percentages.

FIGURE 39.5   A button expanding to maintain its absolute pixel padding on a
high-resolution monitor.

- With **Canvas** selected, in the **Inspector View's Canvas Scaler (Script)** component, specify the **UI Scale Mode** as **Scale With Screen Size**.

- If any issues result with **Button**, reposition it to the upper left-hand corner using the method mentioned earlier.

Problems can still arise if, for example, you are building to a mobile device that automatically reorients between landscape and portrait modes. However, this Canvas configuration is suitable for the majority of screen resolutions.

The next step is to texture the Button. Here, the nomenclature becomes inexact; in Unity, "Texture" refers to a specific image type. The image type used in UI, however, is **Sprite**.

- Into a newly created **UIElements** folder, import the asset **iconRed. png**.

- With **iconRed** selected, specify **Texture Type** as **Sprite (2D and UI)** in the **Inspector View**.

- Select **Button** in the Hierarchy View; click **Apply** when prompted.

- With Button selected, drag and drop iconRed into the **Source Image** field of the **Image (Script)** component in the Inspector View.

- Resize it to 200 × 70 (a percentage of its original resolution of 612 × 212).

- With Button expanded, select **Text**.

- In the **Text (Script)** in the Inspector View, specify **Veranda** as **Font** and **33** as **Font Size**.

- Type **Restart**.

- In the **Hierarchy View**, rename Text as **Restart**, Button as **button-Restart**, and **Canvas** as **CanvasLose**.

In this chapter, we put a UI element into the scene and configured, positioned, and textured (sprited) it. We learned some of the pitfalls of the UI system and how to avoid those pitfalls. We configured the Canvas to accommodate multiple screen resolutions. In the next chapter, we will have **buttonRestart** reload the scene.

CHAPTER 40

UI–PlayMaker Integration

T HERE ARE SEVERAL CONSIDERATIONS that make UI elements unique in terms of State machine integration. In this chapter, we will learn how to make a button function in conjunction with PlayMaker.

What UI does is fairly limited, from a certain perspective. It either informs the player or receives input. What the input does can have dramatic effects of course, but the UI element itself is simply a middle man. This simplicity is reflected in PlayMaker's UI proxy system.

Take, for example, the usual button. Its start State is unclicked and waiting to be clicked. Because this configuration is nearly universal, it can be encapsulated in a standardized Component. This Component, provided by Hutong Games, comes equipped with necessary functionality and parameters helping to bridge the gap between PlayMaker and Unity UI. With a UI element established in Scene and the UI Proxy Full Package already imported (using Ecosystem), PlayMaker integration is a straightforward process:

1. Drag and drop the **PlayMaker UGui** Prefab from **Assets>PlayMaker UGui>Prefabs** into the Hierarchy.

2. Add the appropriate **PlayMaker UGui Proxies** script as a Component to the **UI element**.

3. Add an **FSM** to the UI element and complete the State machine with the appropriate actions.

We want our buttonRestart to have the ability to reload the Scene. We will accomplish that now.

- Open the previous Scene, **Save Scene as... sec3Chap40UIPlay MakerPractice**.

- In the **Project View**, select **PlayMaker UGui>Prefabs>PlayMaker UGui** and drag and drop it into the **Hierarchy View**.

- With **buttonRestart** selected, **Add Component Play Maker UGui Component Proxy** in the **Inspector View**.

- Right-click to **Add FSM**.

- Rename the FSM as **buttonFSM**.

- Right-click to add **State 2**, rename it as **whenClicked**.

- Right-click State whenClicked to **Add Global Transition>UGUI>ON CLICK**.

- Note that ON CLICK, like all other transitions whose names are written in capitalized letters, serves as both transition and action all-in-one.

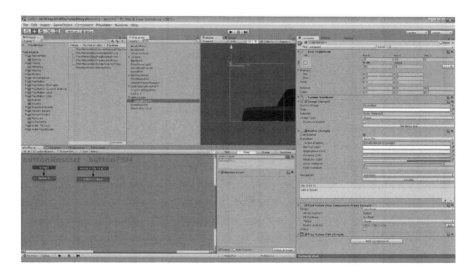

FIGURE 40.1 Shown here is a correctly configured buttonRestart UI element and its associated FSM.

- Save the FSM as template **buttonFSMTemplate**.

- With whenClicked selected and **State** activated in the Control Bar, add action **Restart Level** (Figure 40.1).

The PlayMaker UI proxy system bridges the gap between PlayMaker and Unity's UI in much the same way as its Animator proxy system bridges PlayMaker and Mecanim. In both instances, FSMs are being used to trigger Unity systems. **The PlayMaker UI proxy system is comprised of Unity UI elements, a PlayMaker Prefab, a PlayMaker Component, and the FSM.**

In this chapter, we successfully integrated PlayMaker and UI. Our button now triggers the restart of the Scene. In the next chapter, it is crunch time. The dreaded deadline approaches and we will need to do everything possible to expedite the conclusion of our Project. The final chapter will involve generalized instructions on how to complete the game using previously acquired knowledge and processes.

CHAPTER 41

Crunch Time

A T SOME POINT IN your game project's development, you will multiply eight by the number of days until deadline and realize there are not enough hours in the typical work day. Crunch is what happens when you have to fit more and more work into ever dwindling hours and more and more work hours into ever dwindling days. The game industry is rife with anecdotal horror stories of the time, health, and relationships lost to crunch. Is crunch a necessary evil or just evil? Or, is it actually beneficial, another limitation serving to inspire creative problem solving? Can crunch inspire creativity or is it the result of the process, forth from the temperamental time table lady inspiration keeps? Conversely might a deadline kill creativity, cutting short a flower about to bloom? Are you a philosopher or a game developer? What's with all the questions? Get back to work!

The fact of the matter is crunch happens. Nondestructive overtime can even be a badge of honor for an indie developer. It implies you are not copping out by copying and cloning other games. It also shows that you are self-disciplined and serious about keeping deadlines. With a whole lot to do and only one chapter left to do it in, you are about to earn your badge. It's crunch time!

We should begin by taking stock. Our minimally viable game still needs the following:

1. A **Quit** button for our game over Canvas (**canvasLose**)

2. A win screen (**canvasWin**)

3. A teleportation particle effect

4. A properly functioning cyborgNinja

5. A sword for cyborgNinja and a gun for the player's avatar

6. Rain and rain splash effects

7. A helipad and a way for the player to win

8. An introduction/instructions screen

9. An executable

To really eke out all possible efficiency, it is sometimes best to work backward beginning with the end. That is because the end is the end; we can be assured that the GameObjects that appear last will not need to send messages to any other GameObjects. That serves to minimize the confusion arising from growing interconnectedness. It also means not having to constantly revisit FSMs to update Actions with the names of GameObjects that have yet to be created. There are obvious limitations to this back-to-front strategy, but it is useful here. Our final GameObjects are our win and lose screens, so let's begin there.

- Open the previous scene, **Save Scene as... sec3Chap41 CrunchTimePractice**.

- Select **buttonRestart** and duplicate it.

- Rename the new buttonRestart as **buttonQuit** and Restart as **Quit**.

- Specify its **Pos Y** value as −120.

- Replace its **Restart Level** Action with an **Application Quit** Action.

- In Quit's **Text (Script)** Component, replace **Restart** with **Quit**.

- Into the **UIElements Folder**, import **hitSeeingRed.psd**.

- In the Inspector View, select **Sprite** as its **Texture Type** and click **Apply**.

- With **canvasLose** selected, right-click and select **UI>Panel** (Figure 41.1).

- Note that the Buttons become grayed out.

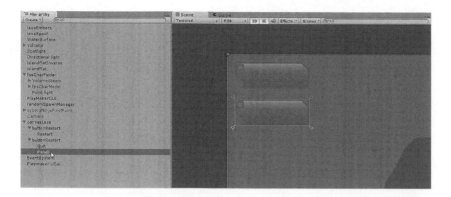

FIGURE 41.1   Panel is listed beneath its siblings in the Hierarchy View and yet rendered before its siblings in Scene View.

Unity's UI has an odd ordering system. The further down in the Hierarchy a Canvas child appears, the higher it is in the rendering order. That means that if **Panel** is the last child in the Hierarchy, then it is the first element to render. As a result, it will cover the buttons; this is problematic. In order for it to render last, we will have to move it higher up the family tree than any of its siblings.

- Click and hold and drag **Panel** upward to reposition it above the other children in the Hierarchy View list.

- Note that the Buttons are no longer grayed out (Figure 41.2).

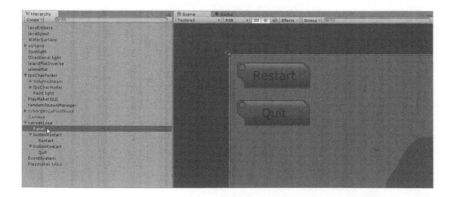

FIGURE 41.2   Here, Panel is listed above its siblings in the Hierarchy View and rendered after its siblings in Scene View.

- In the **Image (Script)** Component, specify **Source Image** as **hitSeeingRed**.

- Deactivate **canvasLose**.

We will now create a win screen. It will be composed of a single text element.

- With nothing selected, right-click the negative space in Hierarchy View and right-click to choose **UI>Text**.

- Rename the Canvas as **canvasWin**.

- In the **Canvas Scaler** (Script) Component, choose **Scale With Screen Size** for the **UI Scale Mode**.

- Rename **Text** as **youWin**.

- Match youWin's parameters with those in **Figure 41.3**.

- Deactivate **canvasWin** (Figure 41.3).

Next, we will implement a teleportation special effect. We want it to play when cyborgNinja teleports in as a result of spawning and when cyborgNinja teleports out as a result of being shot. As a child of cyborg-NinjaPivotPoint, it will activate when cyborgNinjaPivotPoint is spawned.

- Put **Elementals>Thunder>Lighting Spark** into the scene and child it to cyborgNinjaPivotPoint.

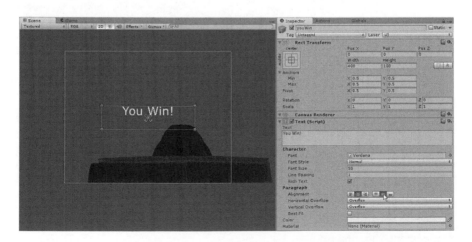

FIGURE 41.3 An illustration of youWin's correctly specified parameters.

- **Add Component Audio Source** to Lightning Spark.

- Put **sndFXSparks** into the **Audio Clip** field.

- **Right-click to Add FSM sparkFSM**.

- Rename the first State to **spark**; **Add Transition FINISHED**.

- Add the Action **Wait**.

- Specify **Time** as **1** and **Finish Event** as **FINISHED**.

- Create a second State called **deactivate**.

- Add the Action **Activate GameObject**.

- Uncheck the **Activate** box.

- Link FINISHED to State deactivate.

By starting with the last necessary game objects, we have avoided amassing mental clutter and needing to repeatedly edit FSMs. However, we were not able to employ this strategy from the very beginning; there were simply too many unknowns at that point. For example, we made FSM AI long before we had the notion to create the teleportation effect using the Lightning Spark Prefab. For this reason, we will have to revisit the AI FSM. Because we want Lightning Spark to coincide with cyborgNinja's exit teleportation, it is from there that we will activate Lightning Spark.

- In **FSM AI**, select State **hit**.

- Add Action **Activate GameObject**.

- Specify **GameObject** as **Lightning Spark**.

Great! Let's repair cyborgNinja. Currently, he runs from the player. This is because when we created fpsCharModel, we deleted fpsCharStandIn and never respecified the dependent parameters. It is necessary to rectify that oversight. Likewise, we will need to fill the slots vacated by the now defunct cyborgNinjaStandIn. While we are there, cyborgNinja will get a sword swinging sound effect.

- In the **randomSpawner** FSM, in the **randomSpawning** State, drop **cyborgNinjaPivotPoint** into all the **None (GameObject)** fields.

- In the **AI** FSM, in the **goTo** State, drop **fpsCharModel** into all the **None (GameObject)** fields.

- In the **attack** State, add **Activate GameObject** and **Audio Play** Actions.

- The GameObject to **Activate** is **canvasLose**.

- The **Audio Play One Shot Clip** is **sndFXSwordSlashes**.

- **FINISHED** should be added as both the **Finished Event** and the State's **transition**.

- Add State **gameOver**.

There are eventualities that we need to head off in this State. One is the cyborgNinja sneaking up and dispatching the player without the player ever knowing what hit him/her. Having spent many long hours sculpting the cyborgNinja, we don't want it to go unseen. We will use **Smooth Look At**. We also want to disable the player's inputs so that the player cannot continue to move or shoot. Deactivation will not work in this instance as it would deactivate the Main Camera as well. We will use **Destroy Component** instead.

- Add the Action **Smooth Look At** to the **gameOver** State; specify that **fpsChar@shooting** look at **cyborgNinjaModel**.

- Add another **Smooth Look At** Action to the **gameOver** State; specify that **cyborgNinjaModel** look at **fpsChar@shooting**.

- Add four **Destroy Component** Actions; **fpsChar@Shooting** should have its **MouseLook**, **FPSInputController**, **CharacterMotor**, and **CharacterController** Components destroyed in that order.

- Note that Unity will report errors during in-editor playtesting that will not occur in the final build; simply unpause playtesting when the "errors" occur.

We also need to prevent the firing and RaycastingBullets FSMs from functioning once the game has ended. Luckily, we had the foresight to give them the same Global Transition. We can kill two FSMs with one Send Event.

- Add the Action **Send Event**.

- Specify **Event Target** as **Broadcast All**.

- **Send Event*** should be **toGameOver**.

- Link **FINISHED** to GameOver.

- Deactivate **cyborgNinjaPivotPoint**.

The cybogNinja and FPS character need a sword and gun, respectively. Weapons are the "HelloWorld" program of modeling; being the first model a model maker makes these models moderately mundane. The models that I do not handcraft I download from the following sites:

- **http://www.turbosquid.com**

- **http://www.assetstore.unity3d.com**

- Paying close attention to copyrights, download one gun and one sword model.

- Import the meshes into the **Meshes** folder and the textures into the **Textures** folder.

- Add the meshes to the scene and child them to their respective hand bones.

- Assign the meshes their textures.

We've long had a rain sound effect but no rain. By now, you should have no problem implementing this yourself, especially since it makes use of our very first template: followGameObjectTemplate (Figure 41.4).

- In Assets, **Water FX Pack>Prefabs** expand **Rain** and rename the second child as **FX_Spray** in the Inspector View.

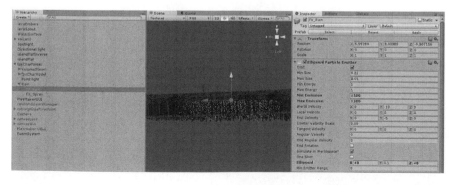

FIGURE 41.4   Shown here are Prefabs configured for use in the scene.

- Note that the Asset will not update until the Scene is saved.

- Child the Rain Prefab to **fpsCharFolder**.

- Apply the process used to achieve the functioning of **VolumeSteam** (i.e., following an **Empty GameObject** target childed to **fpsChar-Model**) to the Prefabs **FX_Rain** and **FX_Spray**.

- Be sure to simplify the process using the **followGameObject Template**.

- In the **Ellipsoid Particle Emitter** of both Prefabs, change the **X** and **Z Ellipsoid** values to 40.

- In the Ellipsoid Particle Emitter of both Prefabs, change the **Min Emission** and **Max Emission** values to at least 1000 (Figure 41.4).

By downloading free audio, model, and Prefab assets, you are smartly having someone else do your work for you. Speaking of which, you are in luck. You have received helipad.unitypackage!

- Into a newly created **Prefabs** folder, import **helipad.unitypackages**.

- Instantiate the **helipad** Prefab into a clearing on the side of **volcano** opposite **fpsCharModel**.

- Recess the helipad into the ground so that **fpsCharModel** can step onto it (this parameter is controlled in **Step Offset** of the **Character Controller** Component).

- Expand the helipad Instance and select **homeBase**.

- Note that the **waitForTrigger** State uses a special **System Events** transition that is both **Action** and **Transition**.

- Note that for **TRIGGER ENTER** to work, the **Capsule Collider** Component's **Is Trigger** parameter must be checked as true.

- Having selected **Edit Instance**, configure State **homeSafe** as seen in **Figure 41.5**.

The final piece of the puzzle has also been made available to you as a Scene. It contains a title screen, backstory, and gameplay instructions

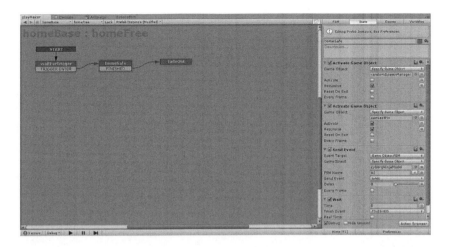

FIGURE 41.5   A properly configured helipad instance.

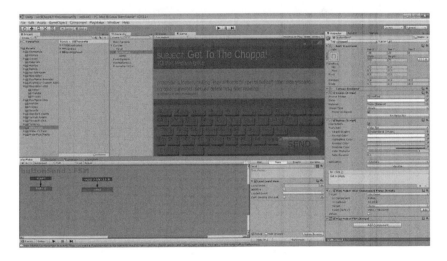

FIGURE 41.6   sec3Chap41TitleScreen is comprised of the textMsgPanel sprite applied to a Panel element and a single button with a single Action: Load Level Num, Level Index 1.

for the end user. Cleverly, these have all been disguised in the form of an in-game text message so as not to disturb immersion (Figure 41.6).

In this chapter, we worked some overtime and lived to tell the tale. In the next chapter, assuming you have playtested and troubleshot your creation, we will build an executable that other people can play.

CHAPTER 42

Build and Conclusion

L ONG AGO, WHEN FIRST introducing File>Build Settings I deferred instruction. We were only as far as the second chapter; I had said that it was unnecessary to know about File>Build Settings until we were ready to Build. *That time, alluded to so long ago is now.* We're finally ready to release our game into the world! To do that, we will create an executable for use on PC. In this chapter, we will learn a process that, while demonstrated for PC, can be applied across multiple builds for various platforms.

To add a scene to a build, it must first be loaded. We will begin by opening the title screen Scene, sec3Chap42TitleScreen (Figure 42.1).

- Load sec3Chap42TitleScreen.unity.

- Import **gameDefaultIcon.jpg** into the **UIElements** folder.

- Along the bottom of the PlayMaker View, click **Preferences**.

- Uncheck **Show State Labels in Game View**.

- **Open File>Build Settings**.

- In the **Build Settings** window, under **Platform**, ensure **PC**, **Mac &
Linux Standalone** is selected.

- Click **Add Current** to add our currently loaded scene to the **Scenes
In Build**.

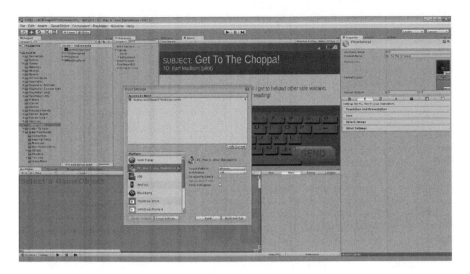

FIGURE 42.1   Build the Settings configuration thus far.

- Click **Player Settings…** to expose the **Player Settings** in the **Inspector View**.

- Customize the **Company Name** and **Product Name** fields.

- Specify **Default Icon** as **gameDefaultIcon**.

- Most of the remaining default settings are sufficient; be aware of what settings are available should something go wrong.

- Load sec3Chap42CrunchTime.unity.

- **Open File>Build Settings**.

- Click **Add Current** to add our currently loaded scene to the **Scenes In Build**.

- In the Build Settings window, click **Build**.

- Select the location you want to build the executable and corresponding **Data** folder (Desktop is convenient for now) to.

- Customize the **File name**.

- Click **Save**.

- Click the executable to playtest your new game!

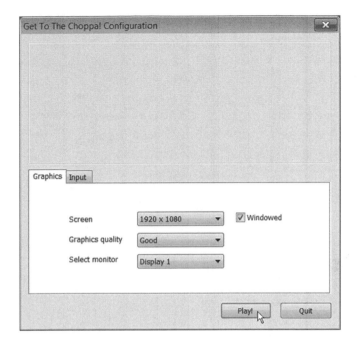

FIGURE 42.2 The game's Configuration window and the all-important Screen resolution settings.

- Note that if the **SEND** button is unresponsive, it is likely due to an incorrect resolution choice made in the executable's **Configuration** window (Figure 42.2).

What seems like the end is really a new beginning for our Project. Its lifecycle begins anew through a process known as iterative development. Iterative development is the process of tweaking and playtesting, tweaking and playtesting, and tweaking and playtesting. Rarely, you will need to overhaul entire sections or mechanics of a game and start from scratch. For our game, iterative development will help determine the best settings (e.g., AI FSM's **Max Speed** parameter), the best placement (e.g., volumeSteam-Target), and the best scale (e.g., cyborgNinja) for our GameObjects. It will also reveal bugs and oversights (e.g., you can currently walk right through the volcano, add a Mesh Collider). While art is never "finished," iterative development will help you to get as close as possible.

We learned how to take our game Project and turn it into a game that we can unleash upon the world. We also learned about the importance of iterative development in this chapter. There is no next chapter as far as this book is concerned. This book's end begins the next chapter in your new life—life as a creator of worlds, compelling characters, and innovative ideas. You are now an indie game developer!

I am excited to see what you create! Feel free to contact me with your creations and be sure to keep in touch through my website, Twitter, Facebook, and e-mail. I am making it a point to post additional resources at those locations; especially at http://nickelcitypixels.com. Thanks for making games with me, it has been an epic journey!

Index

Printed and bound by CPI Group (UK) Ltd, Croydon, CR0 4YY

21/10/2024

01777049-0015